D1503457

Logistics Management

Logistics Management

An Analytics-Based Approach

Tan Miller
Matthew J. Liberatore

BEP BUSINESS EXPERT PRESS

Logistics Management: An Analytics-Based Approach
Copyright © Business Expert Press, LLC, 2020.

First published in 2020 by
Business Expert Press, LLC
222 East 46th Street, New York, NY 10017
www.businessexpertpress.com

ISBN-13: 978-1-94944-384-4 (paperback)
ISBN-13: 978-1-94944-385-1 (e-book)

Business Expert Press Supply and Operations Management Collection

Collection ISSN: 2156-8189 (print)
Collection ISSN: 2156-8200 (electronic)

Cover image licensed by Ingram Image, StockPhotoSecrets.com
Cover and interior design by S4Carlisle Publishing Services Private Ltd., Chennai, India

First edition: 2020

10 9 8 7 6 5 4 3 2 1

Printed in the United States of America.

Dedication

This book is dedicated to my wife Jeanne and sons Lucas and Nate who have been so supportive and put up with me for all these years.

—Tan Miller

This book is dedicated to my wife Mary and my daughters Kathryn, Michelle and Christine for always being there for me.

—Matt Liberatore

Abstract

As we head into the ever-more globalized world of the 2020s, the critical role that logistics planning and operations plays in ensuring a firm's financial well-being escalates in importance almost daily. Furthermore, the role of analytics in guiding both logistics planning and operational activities has spiked dramatically in the last decade, and this exponential growth shows no sign of slackening. As the phenomenon of Big Data has taken hold in the private sector, firms that as recently as 10 years ago devoted minimal resources to large-scale data mining and analytics have reversed course and invested heavily in data analytics.

In this environment, logistics professionals must have at their disposal, and must understand how to utilize, a broad array of analytic techniques and approaches to logistics decision making. Effective use of analytics requires a strong understanding of both fundamental and advanced logistics decision-making techniques and methodologies. Further, logistics professionals must organize and view these analytics-based decision support tools through well-structured planning frameworks.

In this book, based on more than 25 years of logistics industry practice, we illustrate and explain a wide range of practical logistics strategies and analytic techniques to facilitate decision making across functions such as manufacturing, warehousing, transportation, and inventory management. Further, we also describe how to organize these analytics-based tools and strategies through logistics frameworks that span strategic, tactical, and operational planning and scheduling decisions.

This book is intended for logistics professionals to use as a reference document that offers ideas and guidance for addressing specific logistics management decisions and challenges. In particular, it provides explanatory and "how to implement" guidance on foundational analytics that logistics professionals can employ to generate practical insights to facilitate their daily and longer-term logistics management activities. This book can also serve as a valuable resource or secondary text for graduate and advanced undergraduate students. Students will develop an understanding of leading edge, real-world approaches for logistics planning and scheduling, decision support, performance measurement, and other key logistics activities.

Keywords

logistics planning; logistics analytics; logistics planning frameworks; logistics management; operations management; logistics performance measurement; logistics metrics; transportation planning; transportation mode choice decision making; integrated inventory and transportation planning; strategic planning; production planning and scheduling; distribution planning; logistics; hierarchical planning; decision support systems; activity-based costing; collaborative planning, forecasting, and replenishment; the analytic hierarchy process; feedback loops

Contents

CHAPTER 1

Introduction

To introduce a previous book published in 2012, we stated that "in today's competitive global economy, a firm's market position and bottom-line financial performance is closely linked to its logistics performance." Today, as we head into the ever-more globalized world of the 2020s, the critical role that logistics planning and operations plays in ensuring a firm's financial well-being escalates in importance almost daily. Furthermore, the role of analytics in guiding both logistics planning and operational activities has spiked dramatically since 2012, and this exponential growth shows no sign of slackening for the foreseeable future. Examples of this abound as in recent years many firms, both large and small, have launched new *Data Science* or similarly named groups. As the phenomenon of Big Data has taken hold in the private sector, firms that as recently as 10 years ago devoted minimal resources to large-scale data mining and analytics have reversed course. The fear of competitive disadvantage and the promise of gaining competitive advantages through data analytics have stimulated enormous internal investments in labor (i.e., data scientists), hardware, and software across industry.

In this environment, logistics professionals must have at their disposal, and must understand how to utilize, a broad array of analytic techniques and approaches to logistics decision making. Effective use of analytics requires a strong understanding of both fundamental and advanced logistics decision-making techniques and methodologies. Further, logistics professionals must organize and view these analytics-based decision support tools through well-structured frameworks.

In this book, we illustrate and explain a wide range of practical logistics strategies and analytic techniques to facilitate decision making across functions such as manufacturing, warehousing, transportation, and inventory management. Further, we also describe how to organize these analytics-based tools and strategies through logistics frameworks that span strategic, tactical, and operational planning and scheduling decisions. Logistics professionals can use this text as a reference document that offers ideas and guidance for addressing specific logistics management decisions and challenges. In particular, this book provides explanatory and "how to implement" guidance on foundational analytics that logistics professionals can employ to generate practical insights to facilitate their daily and longer-term logistics management activities.

Objectives of the Book

In over 25 years of private industry and consulting experience, we have implemented numerous management decision support and performance measurement systems to manage logistics functions. Further, we have implemented these systems with a keen eye focused on how each system and technique fits into an overall framework for analytics-based logistics decision making in a firm. The implementation of one system or technique typically leads to additional related implementations over time, particularly if the initial implementation generates benefits highly valued by an organization. For this reason, it is critical that one view the development and installation of logistics decision support systems (DSS) within the context of the logistics organization's overall long-term and short-term needs. Our experience has taught us that firms that take this approach make themselves significantly more competitive and agile relative to firms that bounce from one implementation to the next without an overall framework and vision for their logistics decision making processes.

We have several objectives in writing this book. First, we wish to communicate to other logistics practitioners and executives the value of investing in the logistics analytics tools that we describe. These methods served us well in practice, and we strongly recommend them. And as we will illustrate, all the analytics techniques we present can be readily implemented. Our second objective is to raise the visibility and, ultimately, the utilization of these methodologies. In this new age of analytics, one may question whether there remains a need to illuminate further the value of logistics analytics. However, despite the "buzz" about "big data" and the "digital age," and despite the rapid growth in this area during the last decade, many current surveys of practitioners find major logistics decisions still being made without appropriate decision support tools. For example, *Supply Chain News* recently conducted a survey across 23 countries and many industries ranging from "chemicals to manufacturing, metals, telecom, cosmetics, consumer goods, transportation and food." This survey found that:

> Most respondents rely on a combination of spreadsheets (nearly 60%), gut feel (15%) and previous experience (45%) to make supply chain network decisions. Only about 22% use network design software and ... more than half of the professionals assessed indicated that they didn't use some form of advanced analytics to support their network design process. (Further) none of these respondents share data across multiple applications ... in an integrated way.[1]

This leads to our third objective for this book, namely, by presenting analytics tools in easy-to-follow illustrations, we hope to facilitate the implementation of these methodologies by others who wish to utilize them.

A Hierarchical Framework for Logistics Planning

The planning activities and decisions that management must make for the logistics function range from the extremely long run to the short run day to day.[2] Further, the characteristics of these activities and decisions range from those requiring vast resources and managerial time (as measured by cost, required planning inputs, level of risk, and other attributes) versus those requiring relatively minimal time and resources. For example, consider the vast differences in the required inputs for, and implications of, a plant location and sizing decision versus a one-week production line scheduling decision. To effectively address this broad spectrum of management and operational control activities and decisions required in any

---

[1]Supply Chain News (November 7, 2018)

[2]To be clear, this statement applies to supply chain management and all of its functional areas. Because the logistics function, a major subcomponent of supply chain management, is the subject of this book, we focus on this activity and its subcomponents.

major logistics function (e.g., manufacturing), it is necessary to separate the future planning horizon into three buckets:

1. Strategic Planning,
2. Tactical Planning, and
3. Operational Planning

These three planning horizons must be closely and hierarchically linked to ensure aligned decision making, and we will discuss analytic techniques and strategies that facilitate this alignment throughout the book. The interested reader is also referred to Liberatore and Miller (2012) to learn more about the theory and process of hierarchical planning, the types of decisions made at each level of the planning process, and techniques to facilitate the critical linkages required between the logistics management function and a firm's business mission, objectives, and strategies.

Figure 1.1 displays a generic logistics planning framework. We describe this framework as *generic* because it illustrates that the planning activities of any individual logistics function can (and should) be linked to the overall business and logistics strategic planning process of an organization. Examples of significant individual logistics functions include:

- Manufacturing
- Distribution
- Customer service
- Inventory
- Transportation[3]

The definition of what constitutes a major individual logistics function will vary by firm. For example, some firms may consider manufacturing as being separate from logistics. Some firms consider customer service as a component of their logistics organization, while other firms do not. Regardless of how many functions within a logistics organization a firm chooses to define as major individual units, the framework in Figure 1.1 provides a well-defined, holistic organizational approach.

---

[3]The analytics decision support methods and strategies presented in this book will concentrate primarily on these five functional areas.

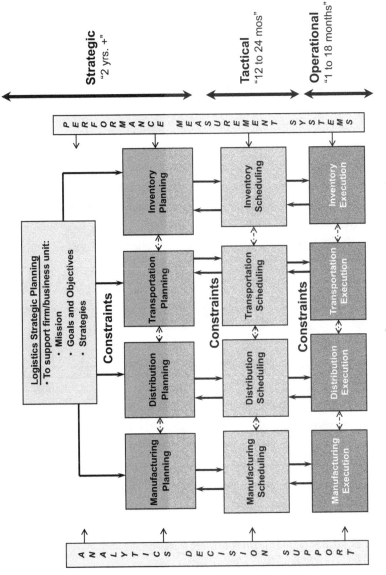

Figure 1.1 A logistics planning framework

5

The logistics planning framework is driven by a firm's business strategic planning process. The goals and objectives developed at the business unit level establish requirements and define capabilities that the logistics organization must provide to support business objectives. This facilitates the next strategic planning process, where the logistics organization formulates its overall mission, goals, objectives, and strategies. The outputs of this process generate high-level requirements and define capabilities that the individual functions within logistics must then deliver. At this point, individual functions such as manufacturing and distribution must initiate their own planning processes to map out the contributions that they will each make in support of the overall logistics plan.

The hierarchical planning framework requires that each individual function delineate the future planning horizon into strategic, tactical, and operational planning buckets. Thus, each logistics function has its own strategic, tactical, and operational planning processes. To illustrate the different types of decisions and management controls exercised at each planning level, note in Figure 1.1 that at the tactical level we use "scheduling" as a function descriptor while at the operational level "execution" is the function descriptor. In practice, at the tactical level one observes both planning and scheduling activities, while at the operational level, planning, scheduling and execution activities all occur. Finally, also note the following in the figure:

1. There are bidirectional vertical lines between the strategic, tactical, and operational planning levels of each logistics function (e.g., manufacturing). The lines flowing from higher to lower levels illustrate that decisions made at higher levels impose constraints or boundaries on decisions made at lower levels. Conversely, lines emanating from lower to higher levels are known as a "feedback loops" in a hierarchical planning system and illustrate the critical need for upward input and communications from lower to upper levels. We will discuss and provide examples of both top-down constraints and bottom-up feedback loops later in this book.

2. There are dashed horizontal lines between the individual functions. These lines illustrate that in practice, interactions in many forms should (and do) occur between individual logistics functions. These interactions can be both formal (e.g., joint planning sessions) and informal (e.g., day-to-day communications).

In summary, the generic logistics planning framework depicted in Figure 1.1 facilitates aligned planning, scheduling, and execution activities all the way down to the operational levels of each individual logistics function.

Analytics Decision Support and Performance Metrics

Now that we have introduced a framework for logistics planning, we turn to the central focus of this book, namely, the role of analytics-based DSS. Analytics decision support methods and systems for logistics planning span a broad array of methodologies and techniques ranging from spreadsheet-based analyses and statistical analyses, to database analyses and data mining, to sophisticated mathematical optimization and simulation models.

Performance measurement systems (PMS) provide managers with indicators of how efficiently and effectively their logistics network is operating. Additionally, good PMS also offer advance warnings or indications of potential future problems. A good PMS is also an absolute necessity to support the planning frameworks of a logistics organization.

Figure 1.1 depicts the integral role that analytics-based decision support and PMS play in a logistics planning framework.

As illustrated, each individual logistics function must have appropriate analytics tools at each level of its planning process. Similarly, each function must also have pertinent performance metrics to monitor its activities. And collectively, the logistics organization must have the DSS and PMS tools required to manage the entire process. A firm with strong analytics/DSS tools and PMS capabilities, but that lacks the appropriate logistics frameworks to organize and utilize these tools cannot succeed. Similarly, a firm with good logistics frameworks, but that lacks the proper DSS and PMS tools cannot succeed. However, a firm with all of these components in place positions itself to conduct effective logistics planning and successful operations.

Logistics Planning: Analytics Methods and Time Horizons

Analytics techniques to support logistics planning and operations provide support for the most highly strategic to the most granular operational short-run decisions. The myriad planning methods and tools that a firm employs to facilitate its logistics decision making collectively comprise a firm's logistics DSS. Figures 1.2 and 1.3 present an illustrative overview of selected methodologies and applications, respectively, frequently found in a firm's logistics DSS.

- **Optimization Models**
- **Simulation Models**
- **Forecasting Models**
- **Statistical Models**
- **Visualization Tools**
- **Spreadsheet Models**
- **Database Tools**
- **Smart Phone Apps (Applications)**
- **Artificial Intelligence Based Tools**

Figure 1.2 Logistics decision support tools

- **Manufacturing and/or Distribution Network Planning**
- **Manufacturing and/or Distribution Network Scheduling**
- **Plant Capacity Planning and Scheduling**
- **Warehouse Capacity Planning and Scheduling**
- **Transportation Planning and Scheduling**
- **Inventory Network Requirements Planning**
- **Inventory Replenishment Scheduling**
- **Network and Location Long Run Demand Forecasting**
- **Network and Location Short Run Demand Forecasting**

Figure 1.3 Illustrative applications of logistics decision support tools

A firm's logistics DSS must address all of its planning requirements from the very long run to the short run day-to-day, as previously noted. Whether a firm is in the initial stages of constructing its DSS or expanding a mature system's capabilities, the ability of a DSS to support the full planning horizon represents a critical consideration. A firm that has excellent *strategic* planning tools but poor *operational* planning tools will struggle with execution. Conversely, a firm with strong *operational* tools but weak *strategic* tools will experience inefficiencies in its logistics operations caused by such issues as inadequate long-run infrastructure planning.

Thus, a comprehensive logistics DSS supports all three planning horizons. Figure 1.4 provides a perspective on the planning horizons and product aggregations found in a hierarchical DSS.

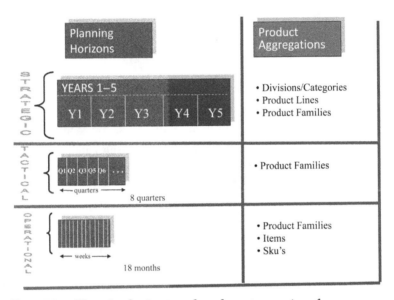

Figure 1.4 Planning horizons and product aggregations for hierarchical planning

Notice that the three planning horizons differ not only in time frame, but also in granularity. While operational planning time buckets range from weeks and months down to hours and shifts, strategic planning time buckets are more typically defined in years or often in one time bucket (e.g., a plan for the next 3 to 5 years viewed as one bucket). In terms of product aggregations, again the planning hierarchy flows from the highly granular at the operational level (e.g., end items) to the highly aggregated at the strategic level (e.g., an entire division or business unit's products). In this book, we will review logistics DSS tools at each level of aggregation.

Scope of the Book

This book presents a broad variety of analytics-based approaches to logistics management. Functional areas addressed will include manufacturing, distribution, inventory management, transportation, and customer service. Within these functional areas, we offer analytical techniques to provide decision support for all planning horizons (i.e., from the operational to the strategic). Further, we describe the role that individual DSS methods play in an overall hierarchical logistics planning framework.

Organization of the Book

The remainder of this book is organized into three major parts followed by a final summary chapter. Part One presents a detailed methodology that logistics professionals can employ to make transportation modal choice decisions on a network. In particular, we demonstrate how and why long-run transportation modal choices (e.g., air vs. ocean) should incorporate network inventory plans and requirements into the decision making process. Thus, Part One is titled "Integrated Inventory and Transportation Mode Decision Making."

This section of the book furnishes the reader with a complete, easy-to-use and easy-to-implement methodology for making transport modal choice decisions. All variables and equations are explained. The discussion guides the interested reader through all the details required to incorporate this straightforward methodology into a ready-to-use, spreadsheet-based transport modal choice DSS.

Part Two, titled "Logistics Decision Support," examines a series of real-world cases where firms utilized a variety of methods to provide decision support for manufacturing, distribution, customer service, and inventory management. A consistent theme throughout this section and the rest of the book is the value of incorporating standardized planning processes into a firm's business logistics operations. To introduce this concept, we briefly review how CPFR (Collaborative Planning, Forecasting, and Replenishment) evolved from a simple forecasting experiment between a manufacturer and retailer into a full-blown industry standard for collaborative planning and operations. We then review several case studies that span logistics decisions ranging from strategic manufacturing and distribution network planning to daily warehouse operations and inventory deployment. Part Two concludes with discussions of several key methodologies such as activity-based costing and hierarchical planning feedback loops that serve numerous logistics decision support roles.

Part Three, titled "Metrics and Techniques for Logistics Monitoring and Control," begins with a presentation of a framework to organize logistics metrics. This hierarchical methodology facilitates maintaining all the logistics metrics of a firm in an aligned, organized approach that monitors logistics performance from the strategic level down to the operational. Next, we illustrate a DSS technique that a firm can implement to construct a customized set of indices to monitor overall logistics performance. The discussion illustrates how a firm can develop weights to gauge the relative importance of each logistics activity to its overall logistics operations. Finally, this section closes with a review of additional techniques for monitoring day-to-day transport and other logistics operations. The book then concludes with a brief summary chapter.

PART I

Integrated Inventory and Transportation Mode Decision Making

CHAPTER 2

Integrating Long-Term Transport Mode Selection into Overall Network Planning

The selection of modes and carriers to serve the transport lanes of a supply chain network has a significant impact on the operations and overall requirements of a network. For example, a firm's decision regarding whether to utilize air or ocean transport to replenish inventory between a supplying plant and a receiving distribution center (DC) located on different continents (e.g., Asia and Europe) will dramatically impact the inventory investment requirements and annual inventory carrying costs of the firm. Therefore, a firm's transportation mode choice selection methodology must integrate inventory requirements and costs into the decision making process. In Chapters 3 and 4, we will focus on analytics-based decision methods for determining the appropriate transport mode and carrier to utilize over individual lanes. First, however, in this chapter, we take a broader perspective and consider how transportation decisions fit into an overall hierarchical network planning approach that spans both short-term and long-term time horizons. To facilitate this discussion, we begin with a brief review of a hierarchical transportation planning framework.

Figure 2.1 focuses on key transportation decisions and how they fit into a hierarchy of decisions. At the strategic level, a firm must design its transportation network strategy to meet the long-term goals and objectives of the corporation. Thus, corporate strategic goals and objectives on customer service levels, order cycle times, transit times, and other

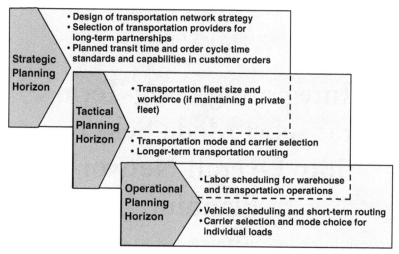

Figure 2.1 An illustrative hierarchy of transportation decisions

strategies with transportation implications must be considered. For example, assume that a firm has an overall strategy to provide the fastest customer order response and delivery in its industry. This dictates that the firm's senior transportation managers must design a network strategy that aligns with this goal. Therefore, they will have to consider factors such as the location of the firm's current and future customer-facing distribution centers, the proximity of those locations to its customer base, the mix of transport modes that can deliver to customers within desired response time objectives, and the cost of alternative distribution and transportation strategies that will meet overall customer service goals.

The high-level transportation network design crafted at the strategic level establishes a framework for the tactical decisions that will follow. For example, as illustrated in Figure 2.1, transportation mode and carrier selection on individual traffic lanes takes place at the tactical level. Here, firms first decide what mode of transport (e.g., air vs. ocean, or truck vs. rail) they will primarily employ on each major transport replenishment and delivery lane. Then, firms utilize tactics such as annual or multiyear bidding processes, whereby the firm selects its carriers for specific lanes for the next 1 or 2 years. These bidding processes typically lead to annual or multiyear contractual agreements that specify rates, capacity requirements, and other key planning variables. Importantly, the modes and carriers selected during this tactical bidding process must possess the delivery speed, reliability, and capacity that the firm's strategic transport network design requires.

Plans and contracts made at the tactical level facilitate the day-to-day selection of carriers to transport freight. Transportation personnel involved in daily operations typically schedule individual carriers on the basis of the approved list of carriers selected for each of their lanes in the tactical planning process. Additionally, at the operational level, one-off decisions will occur in response to occasional issues that may arise, such as the primary carriers for a transport lane not having immediate capacity available for a particular shipment. The number of one-off decisions should be monitored at this level because a high frequency rate over a prolonged period often indicates that plans established at the tactical level require recalibration.

In summary, Figure 2.1 and the illustrative examples discussed offer just a small sample of the numerous strategic through operational decisions required on an ongoing basis to ensure the effective management of a large-scale distribution and transportation network. Nevertheless, this small sample serves to illustrate the hierarchical characteristics of network transportation and distribution planning and provides further context on how to put transportation decisions in the proper hierarchical planning perspective. In the next two chapters, we focus on making mode and carrier decisions at the tactical level utilizing techniques that evaluate the impact of transportation decisions on the "overall" network (i.e., integrated freight and inventory decisions).

CHAPTER 3

Logistics Transport Mode Decision Making

Introduction

In this chapter, we will present an approach to determine the most economic transport mode to ship inventory replenishments of finished goods or materials between two locations. We illustrate the potentially significant costs of not considering both total logistics network annual operating costs and investment criteria in making this decision. The methods presented here are generic in that they can be applied to shipments of products or materials by any transport modes between any locations.

Our hypothetical example assumes that a firm manufactures finished goods inventory (FGI) in a plant in the Far East and distributes these products to customers in Europe from its logistics center located somewhere in Europe. We further assume that the firm supplies make-to-stock products on demand to its customers from this logistics center. Inventory must be maintained at the logistics center to fill orders immediately as customers place them, and it must maintain a safety stock or buffer inventory to cover the variability of demand over the inventory replenishment lead time. Specifically, we consider whether the firm should ship FGI of two illustrative products, A and B, from its plant to its logistics center by either air or ocean.

We begin by presenting the basic data needed for the analysis and then discuss several approaches for addressing this problem, including breakeven analysis, minimizing total annual cost, and the impact of including inventory investment cost and inventory salvage value. All analyses were completed using Excel and are available to the reader on request.

Data

For each transport mode for each product, we require the unit freight costs and the transit time, while for each product we require its value at cost, annual demand forecast, and shipment frequency. We also need to know the cost of carrying inventory, which is based on the opportunity cost of capital for the firm plus the costs related to maintaining a physical inventory, such as warehouse storage and operations, insurance, obsolescence (if appropriate), and so forth. We will assume that the annual inventory carrying cost interest rate is 20 percent, meaning that a dollar's worth of product carried as inventory for 1 year will cost $.20.[1] These data are presented in Exhibit 3.1.[2]

Exhibit 3.1

Data

	A	B	C	D	E	F	G	H
1	E3.1							
2	PRODUCT	MODE	VALUE AT COST ($/UNIT)	ANNUAL FORECAST (UNITS)	SHIPMENT FREQUENCY (DAYS)	FREIGHT COST ($/UNIT)	TRANSIT TIME (DAYS)	INVENTORY CARRYING COST
3	A	AIR	$ 210	23,000	7	$ 52	7	20%
4		OCEAN	$ 210	23,000	7	$ 6	35	20%
5	B	AIR	$ 550	14,300	7	$ 20	7	20%
6		OCEAN	$ 550	14,300	7	$ 5	35	20%

Breakeven Analysis

Breakeven analysis is a commonly used technique for evaluating the modal choice decision. The mode with the higher per unit freight cost (e.g., air) has a shorter transit time and so has a lower cost of carrying inventory in transit. The mode with the lower per unit freight cost (e.g., ocean) has a longer transit time and therefore a higher cost of carrying inventory in transit. Breakeven analysis determines the product cost value at which

---

[1]For more details on how to determine inventory carrying cost, see Coyle et al. (2017).
[2]Note that throughout the remainder of the book, we will often use "carrying cost rate" as a shortened version of the term "annual inventory carrying cost interest rate."

the sum of freight and inventory carrying costs for both modes are equal. PC_{BE}, the breakeven product cost value,[3] is defined as:

PC_{BE} = [freight cost per unit (AIR) − freight cost per unit (OCEAN)]/
[transit time (OCEAN) − transit time (AIR)] × carrying cost rate per day

Exhibit 3.2 presents the results of the breakeven analysis for products A and B. Note that in this and subsequent Exhibits, the Excel formulas applied are shown. The results indicate that the breakeven product cost for products A and B are $2,998 and $978, respectively (cells G3 and G5). Our analysis indicates that if the unit product value at cost for A exceeds $2,998, it is cheaper to ship A by air than by ocean. Otherwise, it is more economical to ship A by ocean. Since product A has a unit product cost of $210, breakeven analysis indicates that it should be shipped by ocean. Similarly, product B's breakeven product cost of $978 exceeds its actual unit cost of $550, indicating that we should ship B by ocean also.

It is important to realize that breakeven analysis only represents a valid technique for evaluating the modal choice decision for a one-time shipment of the product. This will become clearer as we continue our analysis.

Exhibit 3.2

Breakeven analysis

	A	B	C	D	E	F	G
1	**E3.2**						
2	**PRODUCT**	**MODE**	**VALUE AT COST ($/UNIT)**	**FREIGHT COST ($/UNIT)**	**TRANSIT TIME (DAYS)**	**INVENTORY CARRYING COST**	**BREAKEVEN PRODUCT PRICE**
3	A	AIR	$ 210	$ 52	7	20%	$ 2,998
4		OCEAN	$ 210	$ 6	35	20%	
5	B	AIR	$ 550	$ 20	7	20%	$ 978
6		OCEAN	$ 550	$ 5	35	20%	
7							=(D3-D4)/((E4-E3)*(F3/365))
8							=(D5-D6)/((E6-E5)*(F5/365))

---

[3]The total cost (TC) for air (AIR) and ocean (OCEAN) used in breakeven analysis is:
TC(AIR) = average daily demand × transit time (AIR) × product cost × carrying cost rate + annual demand × freight cost (AIR)
TC(OCEAN) = average daily demand × transit time (OCEAN) × product cost × carrying cost rate + annual demand × freight cost (OCEAN)
Setting TC(AIR) equal to TC(OCEAN) and after doing some algebra yields the breakeven product cost PC_{BE}.

Annual Costs

Breakeven analysis indicates that products A and B should be shipped by ocean. A comparison of total annual inventory carrying costs of pipeline and cycle stock inventory plus annual freight costs will validate the ocean option as the preferred mode for both products on the basis of these factors, as shown in Exhibit 3.3 (cells H11 vs. H12, H13 vs. H14). We consider each of these costs in turn.

Pipeline carrying costs are the average carrying costs of inventory while in transit:

$$\text{Pipeline carrying costs} = \text{average daily demand} \times \text{transit time (days)} \times \\ \text{product cost} \times \text{carrying cost rate}$$

In this and subsequent analyses, the frequency of shipments is assumed to be fixed (e.g., every 7 days), so that each shipment contains enough inventory to meet demand during each shipment interval (e.g., 7 days' worth of demand). Cycle stock carrying costs are the costs of carrying one-half of the shipment quantity, since it is assumed that the inventory in each shipment is drawn down at a constant rate, once the shipment arrives at the logistics center:

$$\text{Cycle stock carrying costs} = 0.5 \times \text{shipment quantity} \times \\ \text{carrying cost rate}$$

In our example, the value of cycle stock carrying costs is the same regardless of transport mode, since they depend only on the shipment quantity and not the mode.

Freight costs are simply the annual cost of all shipments, since the entire demand will be met:

$$\text{Freight costs} = \text{annual demand} \times \text{freight cost per unit.}$$

The results of the total cost analysis as shown in Exhibit 3.3 indicate that using an ocean pipeline would yield substantial annual freight savings for both products A and B (cells I3 vs. I4, I5 vs. I6). The higher annual inventory carrying cost of the ocean option (cells G11 vs. G12, G13 vs. G14) reduces somewhat the total potential savings using this mode of transport. The larger inventory carrying cost of the ocean option results from the larger inventory in the pipeline (or in transit) as compared with air (remember that cycle stocks are the same for both air and ocean). The slower transit alternative will always have a larger average level of inventory in transit because each unit of inventory will be in the pipeline longer. Overall, the analysis in Exhibit 3.3 indicates that we can obtain significant annual savings in total freight and inventory carrying costs of $983,896 (cell I12) and $93,832 (cell I14) by shipping both product A and B, respectively, by ocean. However, the total network cost analysis is not yet complete since we have not considered all factors affecting the modal decision.

Exhibit 3.3

Cost analysis excluding safety stock

	A	B	C	D	E	F	G	H	I
1	E3.3								
2	PRODUCT	MODE	VALUE AT COST ($/UNIT)	ANNUAL FORECAST (UNITS)	SHIPMENT FREQUENCY (DAYS)	FREIGHT COST ($/UNIT)	TRANSIT TIME (DAYS)	INVENTORY CARRYING COST RATE	TOTAL FREIGHT COST ($)
3	A	AIR	$ 210	23,000	7	$ 52	7	20%	$ 1,196,000
4		OCEAN	$ 210	23,000	7	$ 6	35	20%	$ 138,000
5	B	AIR	$ 550	14,300	7	$ 20	7	20%	$ 286,000
6		OCEAN	$ 550	14,300	7	$ 5	35	20%	$ 71,500
7									=D3*F3
8									=D4*F4
9									=D5*F5
									=D6*F6
10	PRODUCT	MODE	SHIPMENT QUANTITY	PIPELINE INVENTORY ($)	CYCLE STOCK ($)	PIPELINE + CYCLE STOCK ($)	PIPELINE + CYCLE STOCK CARRYING COST ($)	FREIGHT + PIPELINE + CYCLE STOCK CARRYING COSTS ($)	OCEAN COST SAVINGS ($)
11	A	AIR	442	$ 92,630	$ 46,410	$ 139,040	$ 27,808	$ 1,223,808	
12		OCEAN	442	$ 463,151	$ 46,410	$ 509,561	$ 101,912	$ 239,912	$ 983,896
13	B	AIR	275	$ 150,836	$ 75,625	$ 226,461	$ 45,292	$ 331,292	
14		OCEAN	275	$ 754,178	$ 75,625	$ 829,803	$ 165,961	$ 237,461	$ 93,832
15			=CEILING(D3/(365/E3),1)	=C3*(D3/365)*G3	=0.5*C3*C11	=D11+E11	=H3*F11	=G11+I3	
16			=CEILING(D4/(365/E4),1)	=C4*(D4/365)*G4	=0.5*C4*C12	=D12+E12	=H4*F12	=G12+I4	=H11-H12
17			=CEILING(D5/(365/E5),1)	=C5*(D5/365)*G5	=0.5*C5*C13	=D13+E13	=H5*F13	=G13+I5	
18			=CEILING(D6/(365/E6),1)	=C6*(D6/365)*G6	=0.5*C6*C14	=D14+E14	=H6*F14	=G14+I6	=H13-H14
19	Note: the celing function rounds the result to the next integer								

Safety Stock

A third category of inventory is now considered: safety stock. The purpose of safety or buffer stock is to absorb the variations in the demand during the transit time. It reduces the risk that the item will be out of stock at the logistics center and acts as a buffer in case sales are greater than forecasted. Many inventory systems compute this quantity, and it can be based on a specified level of service in meeting customer demand.[4] For the purpose of illustration, we assume that when replenishment occurs

---

[4]See Coyle et al. (2017) or most other supply chain management or operations management textbooks for an explanation of how to compute safety stock using the normal distribution.

by air, an inventory level equivalent to 2 weeks of sales is required at the receiving logistics center:

$$\text{Safety stock (AIR)} = \text{Annual Demand}/26$$

When replenishment occurs by ocean, we apply a rough approximation of the "Square Root Law"[5] to determine the amount of safety stock for ocean that will provide an equivalent level of service to that set for air:

$$\text{Safety stock (OCEAN)} = \text{SQRT[transit time (OCEAN)}/ \\ \text{transit time (AIR)]} \times \text{safety stock (AIR)}$$

Since safety stock is measured in units, we must multiply it by the product value and by the carrying cost interest rate to determine the carrying cost of safety stock (in dollars):

$$\text{Carrying cost of safety stock (AIR)} = \text{safety stock (AIR)} \times \\ \text{product value} \times \text{carrying cost interest rate}$$

$$\text{Carrying cost of safety stock (OCEAN)} = \text{safety stock (OCEAN)} \times \\ \text{product value} \times \text{carrying cost} \\ \text{interest rate}$$

These formulas are applied to products A and B, and the results are shown in Exhibit 3.4. When safety stock carrying costs are added to the annual cost analysis, the results still favor ocean over air for products A and B with annual cost savings of $937,912 and $19,049, respectively (cells I12 and I14). For product B, the larger safety stock carrying costs for the ocean option greatly reduced the savings previously found when only pipeline and cycle stock carrying costs were considered. These results show the importance of considering all relevant costs in the analysis.

---

[5]Zinn et al. (1989).

Exhibit 3.4

Cost analysis including safety stock

	A	B	C	D	E	F	G	H	I
1	**E3.4**								
2	PRODUCT	MODE	VALUE AT COST ($/UNIT)	ANNUAL FORECAST (UNITS)	TRANSIT TIME (DAYS)	INVENTORY CARRYING COST RATE	TOTAL FREIGHT COST ($)		
3	A	AIR	$ 210	23,000	7	20%	$ 1,196,000		
4		OCEAN	$ 210	23,000	35	20%	$ 138,000		
5	B	AIR	$ 550	14,300	7	20%	$ 286,000		
6		OCEAN	$ 550	14,300	35	20%	$ 71,500		
7							cells I3-I6		
8							Exhibit 3		
9									

	A	B	C	D	E	F	G	H	I
10	PRODUCT	MODE	PIPELINE INVENTORY ($)	CYCLE STOCK ($)	SAFETY STOCK ($)	TOTAL INVENTORY ($)	TOTAL CARRYING COSTS ($)	TOTAL FREIGHT + ALL CARRYING COSTS ($)	OCEAN COST SAVINGS
11	A	AIR	$ 92,630	$ 46,410	$ 185,769	$ 324,809	$ 64,962	$ 1,260,962	
12		OCEAN	$ 463,151	$ 46,410	$ 415,393	$ 924,953	$ 184,991	$ 322,991	$ 937,971
13	B	AIR	$ 150,836	$ 75,625	$ 302,500	$ 528,961	$ 105,792	$ 391,792	
14		OCEAN	$ 754,178	$ 75,625	$ 676,411	$ 1,506,214	$ 301,243	$ 372,743	$ 19,049
15			cellsD11-D14	cells E11-E14	=D3/26*C3	=SUM(C11:E11)	=F11*F3	=G3*G11	
16			Exhibit 3.3	Exhibit 3.3	=E11*SQRT(E4/E3)	=SUM(C12:E12)	=F12*F4	=G4*G11	=H11-H12
17					=D5/26*C5 =E13*SQRT(E6/E5)	=SUM(C13:E13) =SUM(C14:E14)	=F13*F5 =F14*F6	=G5*G13 =G6*G14	=H13-H14

Investment Analysis

Investment decisions typically involve weighting an expected return against the initial investment necessary to generate that return. To evaluate the modal choice decision from a long-run perspective, we define both an initial investment and a return for building the larger inventory pipeline. To accomplish this, we consider the air versus ocean question from an incremental perspective. We know that an ocean pipeline will always require a larger initial investment in inventory than an air pipeline. This results from the fact that the transit time (and therefore days of inventory) of an ocean pipeline will exceed that of an air pipeline. Given that the firm has decided to build an inventory pipeline to support its logistics center, it must, at the minimum, invest in, that is, build inventory for, an air pipeline. The question to be addressed is whether the potential annual cost savings from an ocean pipeline justify the additional investment in inventory to build an ocean pipeline.

In Exhibit 3.5 (cells D3–D6), we summarize the total annual cost calculations from Exhibit 3.4, including the incremental annual cost savings of ocean over air for products A and B of $937,941 and $19,049, respectively (cells E4 and E6). We can view these savings or cost avoidance as the projected annual incremental stream of income associated with the incremental investment in an ocean pipeline. The incremental investment is simply the difference of the total inventory investment of the ocean and air pipelines (cells C4 − C3 and C6 − C5 from Exhibit 3.5). As shown in Exhibit 3.5, the incremental investments for products A and B are $600,144 and $977,253, respectively (cells F4 and F6).

Exhibit 3.5

Investment analysis

	A	B	C	D	E	F	G	H
1	E3.5							
2	PRODUCT	MODE	TOTAL INVENTORY ($)	TOTAL COST ($)	SAVINGS FROM OCEAN	INCREMENTAL INVESTMENT FROM OCEAN PIPELINE	PV OF SAVINGS	
3	A	AIR	$ 324,809.37	$ 1,260,962				
4		OCEAN	$ 924,953.31	$ 322,991	$ 937,971	$ 600,144	$ 2,252,849	
5	B	AIR	$ 528,960.62	$ 391,792				
6		OCEAN	$ 1,506,213.65	$ 372,743	$ 19,049	$ 977,253	$ 45,753	
7								
8			cells F11 - F14	cells H11 - H14	=D3-D4	=C4-C3	=PV(0.12,3,-1*E4)	
9			from Exhibit 3.4	from Exhibit 3.4				
10					=D5-D6	=C6-C5	=PV(0.12,3,-1*E6)	
11	PRODUCT	MODE	NPV OF SAVINGS	PAYBACK PERIOD	ROI	SALVAGE VALUE	PV OF SALVAGE VALUE	NPV OF SAVINGS + SALVAGE VALUE
12	A	AIR						
13		OCEAN	$ 1,652,705	0.64	156%	$ 198,048	$ 140,966	$ 1,793,671
14	B	AIR						
15		OCEAN	$ (931,500)	51.30	2%	$ 322,493	$ 229,545	$ (701,955)
16								
17			=G4-F4	=F4/E4	=E4/F4	=0.33*F4	=F13/(1+0.12)^3	=C13+G13
18								
19			=G6-F6	=F6/E6	=E6/F6	=0.33*F6	=F15/(1+0.12)^3	=C15+G15

With the incremental annual stream of income and the incremental pipeline investment now determined, we calculate a return on investment (ROI), payback period, and net present value (NPV) for the investment on establishing an ocean pipeline. The ROI is defined as follows:

ROI = annual income (savings)/incremental inventory investment

The ROIs for products A and B are 156 percent and 2 percent, respectively (cells E13 and E15). The payback period for the investment is defined as follows:

$$\text{Payback period} = \text{incremental inventory investment}/$$
$$\text{annual income (savings)}$$

The payback periods for products A and B are 0.64 years and 51.30 years, respectively (cells D13 and D15).

NPV is the third financial metric that we will evaluate and is defined as:

$$\text{NPV} = \text{present value (PV) of the income stream over the investment}$$
$$\text{time horizon} - \text{the incremental inventory investment}$$

For the purpose of this illustration, we arbitrarily assume a 12 percent discount rate and a 3-year time horizon. In practice, the investment horizon should generally be linked to either the projected life cycle of the product or a standard horizon defined by the individual firm for investment analyses. Also, the individual firm's opportunity cost of capital represents the proper discount rate for present value calculations.[6]

The NPVs for the incremental ocean inventory investments are computed in two steps. First, we compute the PVs of the three future income streams, which are assumed to be the same values each year. This step requires discounting each of the three income streams back to the present and is accomplished using Excel's PV function. The PV values for products A and B are $2,252,849 and $45,753, respectively (cells G4 and G6). Next, we subtract the incremental investments (cells F4 and F6) from the present values and obtain NPV values of $1,652,705 and $ (931,500) for products A and B, respectively (cells C13 and C15).

The results of the three financial metrics used in our investment analysis show that the incremental inventory investment in the ocean pipeline is advantageous for product A but not for product B. Product A has a very high ROI, very short payback period, and a high NPV. Product B, on the other hand, has an extremely low ROI, a very long payback period, and a negative NPV.

Salvage Value

We now consider the salvage value (if any) of the incremental investment in inventory required to build the ocean pipeline. At the end of a product's life cycle, a firm can generally sell its remaining inventories at

---

[6]See Brealey et al. (2017) or other corporate finance textbook.

some discounted rate. In such cases, a firm may want to include salvage value as part of the investment analysis. For illustrative purposes, we set 33 percent of a product's unit cost as the assumed salvage value per unit. Typically, a firm's financial and/or marketing departments can provide this information. We compute salvage value for ocean pipeline as:

$$\text{Salvage value} = 0.33 \times \text{incremental inventory investment}$$

The salvage values for products A and B are $198,048 and $322,493, respectively (cells F13 and F15 in Exhibit 3.5). Since these values are obtained at the end of the 3-year horizon, they must be discounted back to the present. The PVs of the salvage values for products A and B are $140,966 and $229,545, respectively (cells G13 and G15). Our NPV values previously computed must be augmented by the salvage value PVs, to obtain our revised NPV. These values for products A and B are $1,793,671 and $ (701,955) for products A and B, respectively (cells H13 and H15).

Including the salvage value of the incremental investment in an ocean pipeline will always create a result relatively more favorable to the ocean alternative than if it is excluded from the analysis. However, while the salvage values included in our examples do improve our NPV values, the NPV of the incremental inventory investment for product B is still negative, indicating it is not worthwhile.

Now that we have established an analytical, decision-support approach for inventory pipeline modal choice decisions, we apply this approach to evaluate an example of a more complex transportation alternative.

Effect of Longer Frequency of Shipments

In applying the approach summarized in Exhibits 3.3 to 3.5, it is critical to consider how changes in distribution operations could impact the modal choice analysis. As an example, we now consider the impact of varying the frequency of shipment deliveries on total cost and investment analysis for each transport mode.

Our past analyses assumed that the frequency of shipment arrivals at the receiving logistic center was 7 days for both modes even though the ocean transit times were considerably longer (35 vs. 7 days). As discussed earlier, under this assumption at any one time there would be a series of shipments in the ocean pipeline 7 days apart. As shown in Exhibit 3.3, the air and ocean options have the same size shipments for a given product since both modes must satisfy the same annual demand, and replenishment orders are placed once a week regardless of the transport mode utilized. Since average cycle stock is one-half of the shipment quantity, its value is the same for both transport modes for a given product.

We now revise our assumption about shipment arrivals and assume that the ocean pipeline provides a shipment to the receiving logistics center every 35 days. The effects of this change are seen in Exhibit 3.6. Comparing Exhibits 3.3 to 3.6, we see that for the ocean option the shipment size for product A has increased from 442 to 2,206 and for product B from 275 to 1,372 (cells C12 and C14 in both Exhibits). Larger shipment sizes, in turn, lead to average cycle stocks for the ocean option increasing from 46,410 to 231,630 and from 75,625 to 377,300 for products A and B, respectively (cells E12 and E14 in both Exhibits 3.3 and 3.6). These higher average cycle stock inventories increase carrying costs, and so total annual costs (exclusive of safety stock carrying costs) for the ocean option increase from $239,912 to $276,956 for product A and from $237,461 to $297,796 for product B (cells H12 and H14 in both Exhibits).

Exhibit 3.6

Revised cost analysis excluding safety stock

	A	B	C	D	E	F	G	H	I
1	E3.6								
2	PRODUCT	MODE	VALUE AT COST ($/UNIT)	ANNUAL FORECAST (UNITS)	SHIPMENT FREQUENCY (DAYS)	FREIGHT COST ($/UNIT)	TRANSIT TIME (DAYS)	INVENTORY CARRYING COST RATE	TOTAL FREIGHT COST ($)
3	A	AIR	$ 210	23,000	7	$ 52	7	20%	$ 1,196,000
4		OCEAN	$ 210	23,000	35	$ 6	35	20%	$ 138,000
5	B	AIR	$ 550	14,300	7	$ 20	7	20%	$ 286,000
6		OCEAN	$ 550	14,300	35	$ 5	35	20%	$ 71,500
7									=D3*F3
8									=D4*F4
9									=D5*F5
									=D6*F6

	A	B	C	D	E	F	G	H	I
10	PRODUCT	MODE	SHIPMENT QUANTITY	PIPELINE INVENTORY ($)	CYCLE STOCK ($)	PIPELINE + CYCLE STOCK ($)	PIPELINE + CYCLE STOCK CARRYING COST ($)	TOTAL FREIGHT + PIPELINE + CYCLE STOCK CARRYING COSTS ($)	OCEAN COST SAVINGS
11	A	AIR	442	$ 92,630	$ 46,410	$ 139,040	$ 27,808	$ 1,223,808	
12		OCEAN	2206	$ 463,151	$ 231,630	$ 694,781	$ 138,956	$ 276,956	$ 946,852
13	B	AIR	275	$ 150,836	$ 75,625	$ 226,461	$ 45,292	$ 331,292	
14		OCEAN	1372	$ 754,178	$ 377,300	$ 1,131,478	$ 226,296	$ 297,796	$ 33,497
15			=CEILING(D3/(365/E3),1)	=C3*(D3/365)*G3	=0.5*C3*C11	=D11+E11	=H3*F11	=G11+I5	
16			=CEILING(D4/(365/E4),1)	=C4*(D4/365)*G4	=0.5*C4*C12	=D12+E12	=H4*F12	=G12+I4	=H11-H12
17			=CEILING(D5/(365/E5),1)	=C5*(D5/365)*G5	=0.5*C5*C13	=D13+E13	=H5*F13	=G13+I5	
18			=CEILING(D6/(365/E6),1)	=C6*(D6/365)*G6	=0.5*C6*C14	=D14+E14	=H6*F14	=G14+I6	=H13-H14
19	Note: the celing function rounds the result to the next integer								

As a result, the ocean option does not look as favorable when the frequency of shipment arrivals increases from seven to 35 days. For product A, the savings from selecting the ocean option decreased by $276,956 − $239,912 = $37,044, the increase in annual cycle stock carrying costs (difference of cell H12 from Exhibits 3.6 and 3.3, respectively). However, the cost savings from selecting ocean over air, $946,852, are still considerable (cell I12, Exhibit 3.6). For product B, the increase in cycle stock carrying costs has reduced the savings by $297,796 − $237,461 = $60,335 (difference of cell H14 from Exhibits 3.6 and 3.3, respectively). As a result, ocean now favors air by only $33,497 (cell I14, Exhibit 3.6).

The inventory carrying cost of safety stock remains unchanged when the frequency of ocean shipment arrivals differs (cells E11–E14, Exhibits 3.4 and 3.7). This occurs because the lead time of the replenishment cycle is the same regardless of whether ocean shipments arrive every 7 days or every 35 days. The inclusion of safety stock has reduced the cost advantage of air over ocean for product A to $900,927 (cell I12, Exhibit 3.7), and so ocean remains the preferred option. However, the total cost of the ocean option for product B now surpasses that of air (cell I14, Exhibit 3.7 is negative), and so our decision for product B now favors air. Thus, on the basis of a total cost analysis of both options, in this instance the change in the shipment frequency for ocean, has changed our modal choice decision for product B.

Exhibit 3.7

Revised cost analysis including safety stock

	A	B	C	D	E	F	G	H	I
1	E3.7								
2	PRODUCT	MODE	VALUE AT COST ($/UNIT)	ANNUAL FORECAST (UNITS)	SHIPMENT FREQUENCY (DAYS)	FREIGHT COST ($/UNIT)	TRANSIT TIME (DAYS)	INVENTORY CARRYING COST RATE	TOTAL FREIGHT COST ($)
3	A	AIR	$ 210	23,000	7	$ 52	7	20%	$ 1,196,000
4		OCEAN	$ 210	23,000	35	$ 6	35	20%	$ 138,000
5	B	AIR	$ 550	14,300	7	$ 20	7	20%	$ 286,000
6		OCEAN	$ 550	14,300	35	$ 5	35	20%	$ 71,500
7								=D3*F3	
8								=D4*F4	
9								=D5*F5	
								=D6*F6	

	A	B	C	D	E	F	G	H	I
10	PRODUCT	MODE	PIPELINE INVENTORY ($)	CYCLE STOCK ($)	SAFETY STOCK ($)	TOTAL INVENTORY ($)	TOTAL CARRYING COSTS ($)	TOTAL FREIGHT + ALL CARRYING COSTS ($)	OCEAN COST SAVINGS
11	A	AIR	$ 92,630	$ 46,410	$ 185,769	$ 324,809	$ 64,962	$ 1,260,962	
12		OCEAN	$ 463,151	$ 231,630	$ 415,393	$ 1,110,173	$ 222,035	$ 360,035	$ 900,927
13	B	AIR	$ 150,836	$ 75,625	$ 302,500	$ 528,961	$ 105,792	$ 391,792	
14		OCEAN	$ 754,178	$ 377,300	$ 676,411	$ 1,807,889	$ 361,578	$ 433,078	$ (41,286)
15			cells D11-D14	cells E11-E14	=D3/26*C3	=SUM(C11:E11)	=F11*H3	=I3+G11	
16			Exhibit 3.6	Exhibit 3.6	=E11*SQRT(G4/G3)	=SUM(C12:E12)	=F12*H4	=I4+G12	=H11-H12
17					=D5/26*C5	=SUM(C13:E13)	=F13*H5	=I5+G13	
18					=E13*SQRT(G6/G5)	=SUM(C14:E14)	=F14*H6	=I6+G14	=H13-H14

We now consider the impact of changing the frequency of shipment arrivals on our investment analysis. A comparison of Exhibits 3.5 and 3.8 shows that the modal investment decisions do not change with the increase in the frequency of shipment arrivals but that the financial metrics are negatively affected. Assuming the inventory investment is not salvaged, for product A ocean remains the modal choice, but the payback period increases from 0.64 to 0.87 years, the ROI decreases from 156 to 115 percent, and NPV decreases from $1,652,705 to $1,378,511 (cells D13, E13, and C13, respectively in Exhibits 3.5 and 3.8). The incorporation of salvage value increases the NPV to $1,562,983 (cell H13 in Exhibit 3.8). For product B, air remains the modal choice since there is no payback on the ocean inventory investment and it has both a negative ROI and NPV (cells D15, E15, and C15, respectively, in Exhibit 3.8). The addition of salvage value improves the NPV somewhat, but it is still negative (cell H15 in Exhibit 3.8).

Exhibit 3.8

Revised investment analysis

	A	B	C	D	E	F	G	H
1	E3.8							
2	PRODUCT	MODE	TOTAL INVENTORY ($)	TOTAL COST ($)	SAVINGS FROM OCEAN	INCREMENTAL INVESTMENT FROM OCEAN PIPELINE	PV OF SAVINGS	
3	A	AIR	$ 324,809.37	$ 1,260,962				
4		OCEAN	$ 1,110,173.31	$ 360,035	$ 900,927	$ 785,364	$ 2,163,875	
5	B	AIR	$ 528,960.62	$ 391,792				
6		OCEAN	$ 1,807,888.65	$ 433,078	$ (41,286)	$ 1,278,928	$ (99,161)	
7								
8			cells F11 - F14	cells H11 - H14	=D3-D4	=C4-C3	=PV(0.12,3,-1*E4)	
9			from Exhibit 3.7	from Exhibit 3.7				
10					=D5-D6	=C6-C5	=PV(0.12,3,-1*E6)	

	A	B	C	D	E	F	G	H
11	PRODUCT	MODE	NPV OF SAVINGS	PAYBACK PERIOD	ROI	SALVAGE VALUE	PV OF SALVAGE VALUE	NPV OF SAVINGS + SALVAGE VALUE
12	A	AIR						
13		OCEAN	$ 1,378,511	0.87	115%	$ 259,170	$ 184,472	$ 1,562,983
14	B	AIR						
15		OCEAN	$ (1,378,089)	(30.98)	-3%	$ 422,046	$ 300,404	$ (1,077,685)
16								
17			=G4-F4	=F4/E4	=E4/F4	=0.33*F4	=F13/(1+0.12)^3	=C13+G13
18								
19			=G6-F6	=F6/E6	=E6/F6	=0.33*F6	=F15/(1+0.12)^3	=C15+G15

Summary

The methodology presented in this chapter provides a sound quantitative approach for making inventory transport pipeline decisions. In the next chapter, we will apply this approach to a more complex distribution scenario, both to demonstrate its flexibility and to enhance our understanding. Before doing so, we will offer some summary points based on the analysis presented.

1. *Breakeven analysis should not be used to make an inventory pipeline (modal choice) decision.* Breakeven analysis as presented in Exhibit 3.2 considers freight and inventory pipeline carrying costs and represents a valid technique for evaluating the pipeline decision (air vs. ocean in our example) for a one-time shipment of the product. However, as shown in subsequent analyses, breakeven analysis can generate misleading results since it does not consider all inventory-related costs and the investment aspect of building an inventory pipeline. In our example, breakeven analysis leads to the choice of ocean transport for both products A and B.

2. *The total annual costs of each transport mode should include freight costs and all inventory-related costs: pipeline, cycle stock, and safety stock.* Not including all relevant costs can lead to an inferior pipeline decision. In our example, breakeven analysis (Exhibit 3.2) and a total cost analysis that did not include safety stock (Exhibit 3.3) favored the selection of ocean transport for products A and B. However, safety stock levels will be higher for ocean, the slower transport mode. With the inclusion of safety stock, in our example the savings are greatly reduced when ocean transport is selected for product B (Exhibit 3.4).

3. *The recommended approach for the pipeline decision is to perform an investment analysis.* The slower transport mode (ocean in our example) will require more inventory than the faster mode (air in our case). The difference in the levels of required inventory is viewed as an investment in the slower mode that yields an income stream that is the difference in the annual costs of both transport modes. Standard financial analyses, such as payback, ROI, and NPV can be used to evaluate this decision. In our example, the investment analyses clearly point toward the benefits of choosing the ocean option for product A and the air option for product B (Exhibit 3.5).

4. *Inventory salvage value should be included in the investment decision if appropriate.* If included, salvage value is considered a source of income in the investment analysis and will always show the investment

decision of the slower transport mode, ocean, in a more favorable light than if the analysis excludes salvage value. The potential salvage value of products varies dramatically by industry, by firm, and even by product line within a firm. Thus, one should consider carefully the pros and cons of how to treat salvage value in the pipeline decision. In cases where salvage value plays a decisive role in the decision, this factor should receive increased attention. In our example, the inclusion of salvage value did not affect the pipeline decision (Exhibit 3.5).

A firm may also include salvage value in evaluating work-in-process and raw material pipeline modal decisions. The key question is whether the product or material has some determinable value at the end of the planning horizon.

Computers and electronics are examples of industries where it is appropriate to include salvage value in the decision. For example, it is not uncommon for a computer manufacturer to sell a laptop at a highly discounted price as it transitions to a newer model.

5. *Increasing the time between shipment arrivals will increase cycle stock carrying costs and may change the modal choice decision.* When the frequency of shipment arrivals is the same in two different transit modes, the average cycle stock inventory is the same for both options. However, increasing the time between shipment arrivals in the slower transport mode will increase a firm's annual cycle stock carrying costs and, in turn, its annual total costs, possibly leading to a change in the modal choice decision (Exhibits 3.6 and 3.7). It will also reduce the attractiveness of its larger incremental pipeline inventory as an investment (Exhibit 3.8).

CHAPTER 4

Sensitivity Analysis

Introduction

Sensitivity analysis can and should play a key role in a transport modal choice decision. This technique allows a decision maker to explore how changes in key variables or factors affect a decision. In the modal choice analysis presented in the last chapter, there were a variety of assumptions about values for key variables, such as annual inventory carrying cost interest rate and safety stock requirements. Even if we make accurate assumptions about the values for these variables, it is likely that their values may change over our planning horizon. For example, freight rates change over time, as do interest rates and therefore the firm's cost of capital and carrying cost rate. For this reason, it is critical to perform sensitivity analysis once we have completed the initial modal choice analysis.

If sensitivity analysis indicates that our modal choice decision would remain the same for a wide range of values for key variables, then we can be very confident about our solution. However, if a slight variation in the value of one or more of these variables leads to a change in our decision, then a closer look at our assumptions may be warranted. Further, in such situations we may decide to attach greater importance to nonquantifiable factors excluded from our suggested quantitative approach.

In this chapter, our sensitivity analysis considers changes to several selected variables, including the inventory carrying cost rate, freight cost, and product cost. Changes in the values of any of these variables will change the annual costs of either or both modal choices. Changes in modal annual costs will affect our investment analysis solutions, since the relative annual cost savings will change. Remember that these savings are treated as the income stream in the investment analysis.

Other variables such as changes in salvage value and the length of the planning horizon will not affect the annual cost analysis but may significantly influence the investment analysis results. In our illustrations, we will also consider how changes in the firm's opportunity cost of capital will affect our analysis. The opportunity cost of capital serves as the discount rate in our NPV analysis. In addition, the opportunity cost of capital is a major component of the inventory carrying cost rate. Thus, changes in the firm's cost of capital will affect both our annual cost and investment analyses.

In this chapter, we will also apply breakeven and sensitivity analysis to address how the modal choice analysis can proceed if the value of a key variable is unknown.

Sensitivity Analysis Examples

To illustrate the application of sensitivity analysis, we return to our example from the previous chapter concerning the modal choice decision for product A. Exhibit 3.5 from Chapter 3 clearly indicates that shipping product A by ocean is the best modal decision, since there are significant annual cost savings from selecting ocean as compared with air, the NPV and ROI values are quite high, and the payback period is short. We can add to our confidence that ocean is the best modal choice by performing sensitivity analysis. The four graphs that comprise Exhibit 4.9 demonstrate how changes in the inventory carrying rate affect our four outcome measures: cost savings, NPV, payback period, and ROI. The data for these charts was obtained by using the spreadsheet behind Exhibit 3.5 and then applying Excel's *What If* capability to determine the values for our four outcome measures when the carrying cost rate varies from 5 percent incrementally to 50 percent. We note that the lower and upper limits used for this investment analysis might be a bit extreme but the graphs in Exhibit 4.9 demonstrate that the choice of ocean transport is highly insensitive to changes in the carrying cost rate. In other applications, a narrower range for the carrying cost rate might be appropriate.

Exhibit 4.9

Sensitivity analysis of ocean savings, NPV, payback period, and ROI for product A to changes in the inventory carrying cost rate

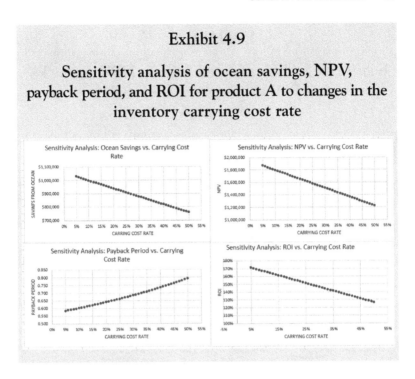

Specifically, even at an extremely high carrying cost rate of 50 percent, the ocean option will generate favorable annual cost savings of $757,928, a substantial NPV of $1,220,771, a short payback period of 0.792 years, and a very high ROI of 126 percent. Further analysis shows that for every 1 percent increase in the carrying cost rate, ocean savings decrease by $6,001, NPV drops by $14,414, the payback period increases on average only by about 0.005 years, or about 2 *days,* and ROI drops by 1 percent. These results indicate that we can have confidence that even if interest rates change significantly or if we have under- or overestimated the carrying cost rate, the decision to ship product A by ocean would be the best choice.

Exhibit 4.10 indicates that similar results occur when a sensitivity analysis of the freight rate cost per unit for product A is conducted. The freight rate for product A could increase by a factor of 2.5 times, and the ocean alternative would still generate ocean savings of $730,971. Further analysis shows that for every $0.25 increase in product A's unit freight cost, ocean savings decrease by $5,750, NPV drops by $13,811, payback period increases on average by about 2 *days,* and ROI drops by 1 percent.

Exhibit 4.10

Sensitivity analysis of ocean savings, NPV, payback period, and ROI to changes in the freight cost for product A

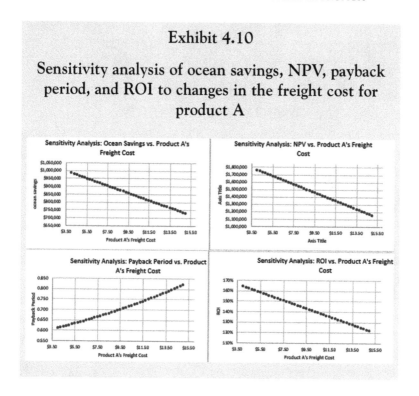

As shown in Exhibit 4.11, sensitivity analysis also reveals that the ocean transit option still yields significant annual cost savings of $755,070 even if product A's cost increases fourfold to $530. At this elevated product cost, the financial metrics are still good, with an NPV of $298,902, a payback period of 2.006 years, and a 50 percent ROI. As product A's cost increases, the incremental investment required for the ocean pipeline increases since the value of the inventory increases. The annual savings decrease because the carrying costs of the more expensive inventory increase. Exhibit 4.11 indicates that despite the higher investment and lower annual savings associated with higher product A costs, NPV, payback period, and ROI remain favorable over a wide range of costs. For every increase of $20 in product A's cost, ocean savings decrease by $11,431 and NPV decreases by $84,613, while payback period incrementally increases initially from 23 days to a high of 38 days, and ROI incrementally decreases by 38 to 3 percent.

Exhibit 4.11

Sensitivity analysis of oceans savings, NPV, payback period, and ROI to changes in product A's cost

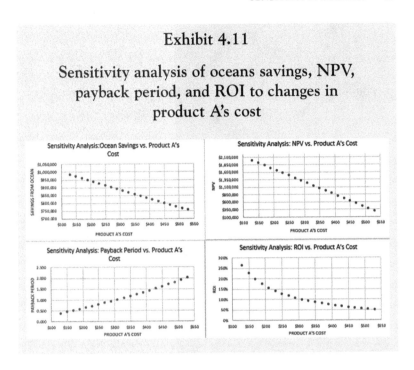

Our final illustration of sensitivity analysis evaluates how changes to the firm's inventory carrying cost rate and the opportunity cost of capital could affect the modal choice decision. We allow the cost of capital to range from 10 to 20 percent and assume that the inventory carrying cost rate changes by the same percentage. Since the base case cost of capital and inventory carrying cost rate are 12 and 20 percent, respectively, the inventory carrying cost rate is set as the opportunity cost of capital plus 8 percent.

The results of the sensitivity analysis for the opportunity cost of capital are shown in Exhibit 4.12. Even for high values of the cost of capital, all financial metrics are favorable. The results show that with each half-percent increase in the cost of capital, ocean savings decrease by $3,001, NPV decreases first by $28,039 and finally by $21,148, payback period decreases by less than 1 day, and ROI decreases by 0.5 percent.

Sensitivity Summary

Sensitivity analysis should be performed on those variables that can have a major effect on the modal choice decision. We performed sensitivity

Exhibit 4.12

Sensitivity analysis of ocean savings, NPV, payback period, and ROI for product A to changes in the opportunity cost of capital

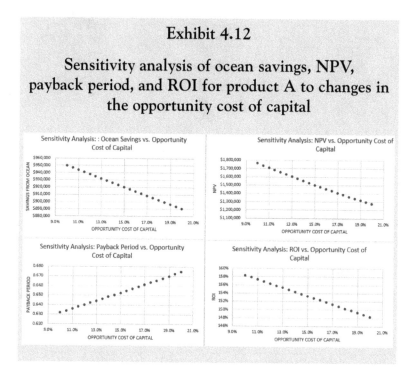

analysis over four key variables: carrying cost rate, freight cost of product A, the unit cost of product A, and the opportunity cost of capital. In our illustrations, we found that the initial decision to ship by ocean remained unchanged over a wide range of values for each of these variables. These findings substantially enhance our confidence in making the incremental inventory investment in product A's ocean pipeline. Sensitivity analysis indicates that even if conditions change (e.g., interest rates rise) or if we have miscalculated one or more of the variables (e.g., the cost of product A), our modal choice decision is unaffected. This is the power of sensitivity analysis and the reason for which this technique should always be incorporated into the decision-making process.

We hasten to point out that sensitivity analysis will not always yield such clear support for the initial decision. In cases where sensitivity analysis reveals that the transport modal choice would change with minor perturbations in the values of key variables, additional analysis is generally required. For example, if sensitivity analysis shows that a relatively small change in one variable can sway a decision in either direction, that variable should be investigated more closely to reach a decision. Alternatively, if sensitivity analysis shows that the results will vary from one mode to another with only minor variations in several variables, one may need to attach more weight to nonquantitative factors within the decision-making process.

The Modal Choice Decision When Some Information Is Unavailable

In some situations, not all of the data required by the modal choice decision-making approach described in the previous chapter will be available. In such circumstances, it is often possible to perform enough of the analysis to make an informed decision. Safety stock requirements at the receiving logistics center offer perhaps the best example of data that might not be available. Firms that lack sophisticated inventory management systems may have difficulty ascertaining their safety stock requirements under alternative replenishment modes. For illustrative purposes, we now consider how to analyze the modal choice decision in the absence of safety stock data.

We return to our modal choice example and the results found in Exhibit 3.3. Without a consideration of safety stock, ocean is the preferred transit mode for products A and B on the basis of the total of freight costs and pipeline and cycle stock carrying costs. However, we know that ocean will require more safety stock than air since it is the slower transit mode and so has a longer lead time for inventory replenishment. We can perform a type of breakeven analysis to determine how much greater the safety stock requirements could be under ocean replenishment before the decision would change to air. This analysis will improve our understanding of the impact of safety stock on our decision.

The breakeven point between ocean savings and the incremental carrying costs of safety stock investment can be determined as follows. First, the formula for the incremental carrying cost of safety stock is simply:

$$\text{Incremental carrying costs of safety stock} = \text{carrying cost rate} \times \text{product cost} \times \text{safety stock units}$$

Next, this formula is set equal to the ocean savings:

$$\text{Carrying cost rate} \times \text{product cost} \times \text{safety stock units} = \text{ocean savings}$$

Solving for safety stock units yields:

$$\text{Safety stock units} = \text{ocean savings}/(\text{carrying cost rate} \times \text{product cost})$$

We can then convert the safety stock units into weeks of supply:

$$\text{Weeks of supply} = \text{safety stock units}/(\text{annual demand}/52)$$

These formulas are implemented in Exhibit 4.13 and show that for product A, safety stock under ocean replenishment would have to exceed the safety stock requirements under air by 23,426 units of inventory before the annual savings of shipping by ocean would be depleted. This amount of safety stock represents 53 weeks' worth of inventory on the basis of the unit cost and annual sales forecast for product A. In practice, our decision to transport product A could switch to air from ocean significantly before the ocean savings are eliminated, although the savings are quite large in terms of incremental safety stock. However, this analysis provides a valuable insight into the impact of incremental safety stock.

In the case of product B, Exhibit 4.13 shows that the annual ocean savings of $93,832 would be eliminated by 853 units of safety stock or 3.1 weeks of supply. The small amount of safety stock supply at breakeven shows that the decision to select ocean over air for product B is less clear-cut.

Exhibit 4.13

Safety stock breakeven analysis

	A	B	C	D	E	F	G	H	I	J
1	E4.13									
2	PRODUCT	MODE	VALUE AT COST ($/UNIT)	ANNUAL FORECAST (UNITS)	INVENTORY CARRYING COST RATE (%)	TOTAL FREIGHT + PIPELINE + CYCLE STOCK CARRYING COSTS ($)	SAVINGS FROM OCEAN ($)	INCREMENTAL UNITS OF SAFETY STOCK	WEEKS OF SUPPLY	
3	A	AIR	$ 210	23,000	20%	$ 1,223,808				
4		OCEAN	$ 210	23,000	20%	$ 239,912	$983,896	23426	53.0	
5	B	AIR	$ 550	14,300	20%	$ 331,292				
6		OCEAN	$ 550	14,300	20%	$ 237,461	$ 93,832	853	3.1	
7			from Exhibit 3.3 cells C3 - C6	from Exhibit 3.3 cells D3 - D6	from Exhibit 3.3 cells H3 - H6	from Exhibit 3.3 cells H11 - H14				
8							=F3-F4	=G4/(E4*C4)	=H4/(D4/52)	
9										
10							=F5-F6	=G6/(E6*C6)	=H6/(D6/52)	

A second analysis designed to provide insight into the incremental safety stock question considers how large a safety stock investment we could make and still achieve an acceptable ROI. For the purpose of illustration, we assume that if the ROI of the ocean option drops below 30 percent, then we will ship product A by air instead of by ocean. We recall from the previous chapter that

$$\text{ROI} = \text{annual income (savings)/incremental inventory investment}$$

Our savings will be reduced by the carrying cost of the safety stock, so

$$\text{Annual savings} = \text{savings without safety stock} - \text{carrying cost rate} \times \text{product cost} \times \text{safety stock units}$$

Our incremental inventory investment will be increased by the cost of the safety stock:

$$\text{Incremental inventory investment} = \text{incremental inventory investment without safety stock} + \text{product cost} \times \text{safety stock units}$$

Applying the formula for ROI,

$$(\text{Savings without safety stock} - \text{carrying cost rate} \times \text{product cost} \times \text{safety stock units})/(\text{incremental inventory investment without safety stock} + \text{product cost} \times \text{safety stock units})$$
$$= \text{minimum acceptable or target ROI}$$

After some algebra,

$$\text{Safety stock units} = (\text{savings without safety stock} - \text{target ROI} \times \text{incremental inventory investment without safety stock})$$
$$[\text{product cost} \times (\text{carrying cost rate} + \text{target ROI})]$$

Exhibit 4.14 indicates that we could invest in an additional 8,312 units of safety stock for product A, or 18.8 weeks of supply, and still achieve a 30 percent ROI. Given that the inventory replenishment time by ocean is only 5 weeks, we would probably feel quite confident that ocean would be the economic modal choice for product A even after accounting for its incremental safety stock requirements. For product B, there is no amount of safety stock that can result in a 30 percent ROI, and hence air would be the preferred transit mode.

Exhibit 4.14

Target ROI breakeven analysis

	A	B	C	D	E	F	G	H	I	J	K	L
1	E4.14											
2	PRODUCT	MODE	VALUE AT COST ($/UNIT)	ANNUAL FORECAST (UNITS)	INVENTORY CARRYING COST RATE (%)	INVENTORY INVESTMENT WITHOUT SAFETY STOCK ($)	INCREMENTAL OCEAN INVESTMENT WITHOUT SAFETY STOCK	TOTAL FREIGHT + PIPELINE + CYCLE STOCK CARRYING COSTS ($)	SAVINGS FROM OCEAN ($)	TARGET ROI	SAFETY STOCK UNITS AT TARGET ROI	WEEKS OF SUPPLY
3	A	AIR	$ 210	23,000	20%	$ 139,040		$ 1,223,808				
4		OCEAN	$ 210	23,000	20%	$ 509,561	$ 370,521	$ 239,912	$983,896	30%	8312	18.8
5	B	AIR	$ 550	14,300	20%	$ 226,461		$ 331,292				
6		OCEAN	$ 550	14,300	20%	$ 829,803	$ 603,342	$ 237,461	$ 93,832	30%	NA	NA
7			from Exhibit 3.	from Exhibit 3.	from Exhibit 3.3	from Exhibit 3.3		from Exhibit 3.3				
8			cells C3 - C6	cells D3 - D6	cells H3 - H6	cells F11 - F14	=F4-F3	cells H11 - H14	=H3-H4	=(I4-J4*G4)/(C4*(E4+J4))	=K4/(D4/52)	
9												
10						=F6-F5			=H5-H6	NA		NA

We can extend this analysis and explore the sensitivity of ROI to product A's safety stock investment, as shown in Exhibit 4.15. The impact on ROI per additional $1,000 in safety stock investment is very large for low levels of safety stock but diminishes rapidly, and after $5,000 the decrease in ROI ranges from 10 percent down to 1 percent.

Exhibit 4.15

Sensitivity analysis: ROI vs. safety stock investment for product A

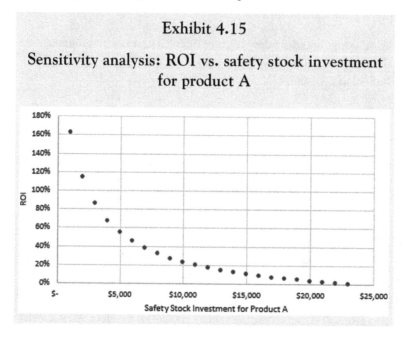

Missing Data Analysis Summary

We have performed breakeven and sensitivity analyses to investigate the impact of an unknown variable, safety stock, on the modal choice decision. Similar approaches can be applied if other variables are unknown. Transport managers must often make important decisions under such circumstances, and this approach can address this type of data gap.

Final Note: Using Sensitivity Analysis to Sell Transport Mode Decisions

Selling the wisdom of a transport modal strategy to the key managers of an organization is a critical task for the transport decision maker, and sensitivity analysis can play a key role in this process. A manager who offers a transport modal strategy supported by thorough sensitivity analysis will demonstrate a strong grasp of this complex decision. This approach serves to convince others that one has not fallen victim to a myopic viewpoint in the solution approach. In particular, the transport decision maker will demonstrate that the suggested solution has addressed many elements of uncertainty (such as interest rates and inventory carrying costs) associated with modal choice strategies.

Sensitivity analysis also allows other managers to participate in the transport decision-making process and can facilitate improved consensus and support for your decision. For example, soliciting other managers' opinions in a give-and-take discussion on what values are most appropriate for key assumptions is one technique that can often generate discussion and ultimate agreement with the transport modal strategy.

Finally, sensitivity analysis can provide the vehicle (no pun intended!) to help senior managers understand the basics of the modal choice methodology. To understand and participate in a sensitivity analysis discussion, one must at least understand the basics of how the key variables in our methodology are used to generate solutions. Thus, a transportation manager selling a modal transport strategy can preface a sensitivity analysis discussion by briefly reviewing the methodology used to arrive at the solutions being pitched to other managers. This will enhance other managers' level of confidence in the transport mode solutions that are presented to them.

PART II
Logistics Decision Support

CHAPTER 5

Introduction

Part Two of this book examines a wide range of tools and methodologies frequently employed to provide decision support for network design, manufacturing, inventory management, and customer logistics. Although the techniques and illustrative cases discussed focus on the aforementioned functions and their processes, the methodologies reviewed also apply and are commonly utilized in related functional areas (e.g., procurement). In keeping with the general theme of this book, our discussion will emphasize an integrated, cross-functional approach in the decision support tools and cases presented.

Standardized Logistics Business Processes

An essential characteristic found in any firm with a strong logistics decision support infrastructure is that the firm has successfully instituted a set of key *standardized* logistics business processes. Further, the firm rigorously adheres to a standardized schedule by which it runs these business processes. Some processes may need to take place once a month, while for others a frequency of once a quarter, once a year or some other interval may be appropriate. The purpose, complexity, and resource requirements of a process will dictate its proper frequency. For example, most firms update their strategic manufacturing and/or distribution network design plans no more than once a year, or perhaps even once every 18 to 24 months. The key point is that the process has a standardized schedule and format and that the firm strictly adheres to its established schedule. Of course, circumstances may occasionally require that a firm conduct an extra iteration of a standardized process before its next scheduled run time (e.g., a manufacturing firm that suddenly experiences a major unanticipated capacity crunch just 6 months into its annual planning cycle).

Importantly, developing and maintaining standardized logistics decision support processes positions a firm to rapidly execute a one-off planning exercise in response to a major unforeseen issue such as a sudden network capacity crunch. In short, standardized processes enhance a firm's agility and responsiveness. A firm lacking such processes cannot respond as quickly, efficiently, or effectively.

Collaborative Planning, Forecasting, and Replenishment: An Example

It is self-evident that standardizing a logistics business process and conducting it on a set calendar schedule ensures that the activity occurs. But why is this important and what are the benefits of standardization? First, as just discussed, this approach improves a firm's agility and responsiveness. Now to explore these questions further, let's briefly consider and glean insights from a well-known logistics process, namely, CPFR (Collaborative Planning, Forecasting, and Replenishment).

CPFR originated from the initial efforts in 1995 of two firms, Warner-Lambert (WL) and Walmart, to improve the accuracy of forecast sales of Listerine Mouthwash at Walmart stores.[1] WL produced Listerine, and Walmart purchased and then sold Listerine. Both firms were independently forecasting expected Walmart store sales of this product, and they decided to collaborate on the forecasting process. Initially, their collaboration took the form of a simple exchange of Excel-based spreadsheet forecasts that each firm independently generated monthly. These exchanges led to a monthly sharing of both forecasts and qualitative insights between personnel at both firms. Within 12 to 18 months, both firms agreed that their collaborative process had yielded a significant improvement in forecast accuracy and, as a result, had facilitated improved inventory utilization. This initial success motivated the firms to embark on a journey to formalize and expand the process over the next several years. Since this pioneering effort in 1995 between these two firms, this initial informal process has evolved and flourished into what logistics professionals today call CPFR. CPFR is now a heavily utilized, well-documented industry

---

[1] See Coyle et al. (2017) for additional discussion of both CPFR and its origins.

logistics process for collaboration in which firms plan and execute activities ranging from daily operations to long-term logistics strategies.

Insights from CPFR's Development and Evolution

CPFR originated as a simple exchange of rudimentary spreadsheets between two firms and, over several decades, evolved into a foundational logistics planning process. Figure 5.1 depicts the expansive range of activities conducted under the umbrella of CPFR.

What lessons and guidance does the evolution of CPFR offer? How can we relate these lessons to the individual firm level?

1. First, after some preliminary experimentation, WL and Walmart realized they had to standardize their forecast exchange process. Forecasts and spreadsheets were exchanged monthly. The firms established

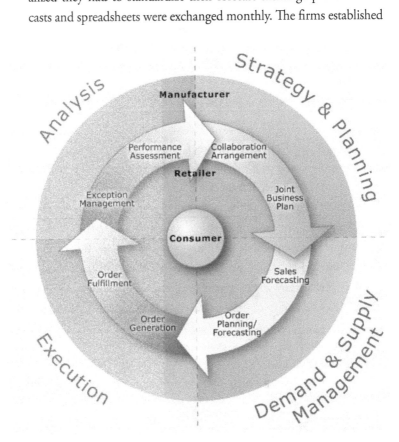

Figure 5.1 CPFR key activities

Source: VICS (Voluntary Interindustry Commerce Standards)

a monthly schedule, assigning specific days of the month for each component of their process. (For example: business day 4—exchange initial forecasts; business day 6—hold a conference call to fine-tune and synchronize initial forecasts; business day 8—publish finalized monthly forecast.)

2. Second, the firms initiated the process with clear, short-term objectives, namely, to improve forecast accuracy and thereby facilitate improved inventory utilization.

3. Third, and related to #2, although the firms had broader plans for collaboration from the outset, they started small—that is, collaborating on and improving their collective forecast accuracy on just one product, Listerine.

4. Finally, by first successfully developing and standardizing a very well-defined process that was narrow in scope, the firms set the stage for the successful development of a much broader, expansive process that ultimately yielded far greater long-term benefits.

CPFR today looks vastly different than the simple experiment WL and Walmart conducted over two decades ago. As the two firms' initial success became public, numerous other firms began similar efforts. Major logistics/supply chain professional organizations such as VICS[2] became champions of CPFR and dramatically expanded the breadth and depth of this process. Commercial software firms developed programs to support CPFR, and so on. In short, CPFR has become an internationally recognized, cornerstone process of customer logistics, utilized by hundreds of Fortune 500 and smaller firms alike. Nevertheless, the insights gleaned from the initial WL/Walmart process still remain valuable today, and we will explore these and other lessons learned in the logistics cases to follow.

---

[2]VICS (the Voluntary Interindustry Commerce Standards or Solutions) Association describes its work as follows.

VICS has enabled companies in the retail and consumer-focused industries to eliminate billions of dollars of waste and delay. By creating voluntary guidelines, often referred to as "standards," VICS has created new best practices that ultimately lead to lower costs and better availability of products for consumers.
Source: Supply Chain24/7 website. (Note that in 2013, VICS merged with the GS1 US organization, and more information is available at www.gs1us.org.)

Outline of Part Two

In the remainder of Part Two, we first review several manufacturing and distribution decision support cases, and then explore several inventory management-related cases. Next, we illustrate techniques for incorporating feedback loops into network planning and inventory management. Part Two concludes with a discussion of activity-based costing and the critical role it plays in logistics management.

CHAPTER 6

Manufacturing and Distribution Decision Support

Introduction

Manufacturing and distribution planning and scheduling frameworks and their components can address an extremely broad range of management activities, from scheduling a single operation of one plant or distribution center to planning and scheduling operations over an entire global network. The introduction in Chapter 1 of a hierarchical planning framework described three broad planning levels (the strategic, tactical, and operational) that address a complex set of linked but different decisions. These decisions differ across many dimensions, including length of planning horizon, level of planning detail, risks and costs of the decisions, and long-term impact of the decisions. Now let's consider several key analytics decision support processes and tools used to facilitate manufacturing and distribution decisions at these different levels.

Strategic, Tactical, and Operational Manufacturing and Distribution Network Modeling

Figure 6.1 presents a hierarchical manufacturing and distribution (HMD) planning framework. At this point in the planning process, business unit strategic plans have been developed and approved, as have the high-level strategic plans of the overall logistics organization. Now, the manufacturing and distribution functions commence their own strategic planning processes to support the overall logistics and business unit strategies.

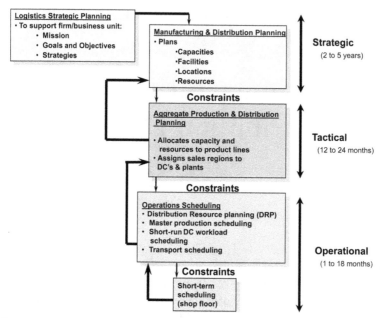

Figure 6.1 Hierarchical manufacturing and distribution planning framework

At the strategic planning level, manufacturing must address such issues as planned production capacity levels for the next two years and beyond, the number of facilities it plans to operate, their locations, the resources it will assign to its manufacturing operations, and numerous other important long-term decisions. Similar decisions must be made for distribution facilities and resources. Decisions made at the strategic level place constraints on the tactical planning level. At the tactical level, typical planning activities include the allocation of capacity and resources to product lines for the next 12 to 24 months, aggregate planning of workforce levels, the development or fine-tuning of distribution plans, and numerous other activities. Within the constraints of the firm's manufacturing and distribution infrastructure (an infrastructure determined by previous strategic decisions), managers make tactical planning decisions designed to optimize the use of the existing infrastructure. Planning decisions carried out at the tactical level impose constraints on operational planning and scheduling decisions. At this level, activities such as distribution resource planning (DRP), rough cut capacity planning, master production scheduling, shop floor control scheduling, and many other decisions occur.

The HMD framework presented in Figure 6.1 is generic in that although individual HMD systems will differ by firm, most systems are designed within this or a similar general framework. Figure 6.2 recaps some illustrative generic decisions that an HMD system constructed within this framework will generally address and displays how these decisions fit into a planning hierarchy. As several of the illustrative decisions in Figure 6.2 imply, HMD systems typically extend beyond a firm's internal operations to include decisions about suppliers and customers.

A Case Study of a Hierarchical Manufacturing and Distribution Planning Framework Implementation

The case study of a HMD presented in this section is based on an implementation that the authors led at American Olean Tile Company (AO).[3] This general framework was later implemented at other firms (e.g., WL).[4] The planning and scheduling components of this HMD represent key

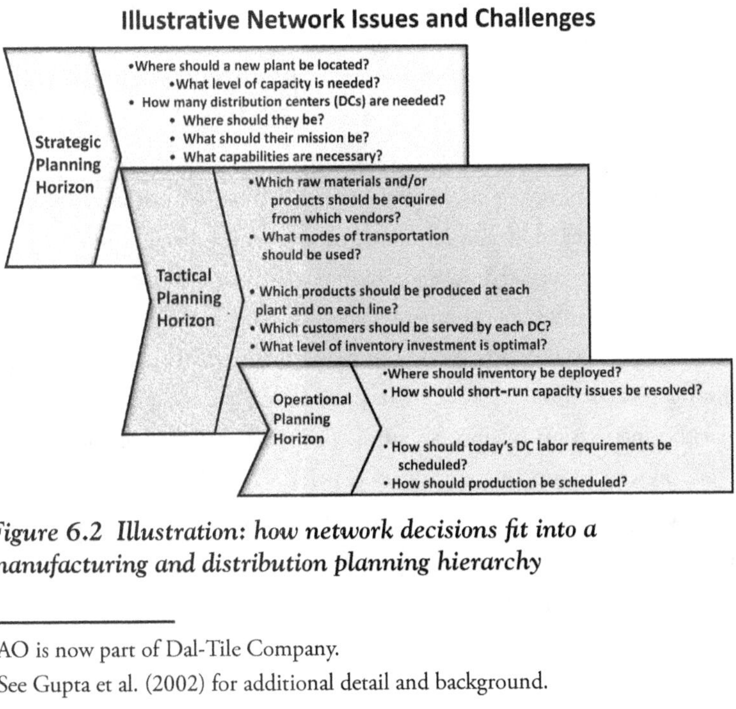

Illustrative Network Issues and Challenges

Figure 6.2 *Illustration: how network decisions fit into a manufacturing and distribution planning hierarchy*

---

[3]AO is now part of Dal-Tile Company.
[4]See Gupta et al. (2002) for additional detail and background.

decision support tools that we recommend for virtually all manufacturing and distribution environments.

AO manufactured a wide variety of ceramic wall and floor tile products, as well as elaborate mural designs, and the firm sold all of its products nationally. At the time it implemented its HMD, AO operated eight factories located across the United States, from New York to California, that supplied approximately 120 sales distribution points (SDPs), which consisted of a combination of sales territories and company-owned stores. Each manufacturing facility had a finished goods warehouse located adjacent to the plant. These factories utilized several different production processes, all of which began with a crushing and milling procedure, and which eventually led to the firing of tile in large kilns. AO produced three basic lines of tile products: (1) glazed tile, (2) ceramic mosaics, and (3) quarry tile.

As the firm's network grew, the lack of coordination between manufacturing planning and distribution planning had become an increasingly significant problem for the firm. For example, AO frequently found itself unnecessarily shipping finished goods inventory (FGI) back and forth between distribution centers because manufacturing and distribution planned their operations independently. This situation eventually prompted AO's management to sponsor a project to address this planning problem. Initially, the program was chartered simply to integrate the annual production and distribution planning processes. However, shortly after the project began, it became clear that AO would not reap the full benefits from integrated annual plant, product, and distribution assignments if it did not also ensure that alignment existed between short-term scheduling and inventory control decisions and annual plans. Thus, AO's management commissioned the development of a full-scale HMD planning system. The objective of implementing this system was to improve the integration of annual production and distribution planning, short-term scheduling, and inventory control.

The designers of AO's HMD system implemented it with the intent that their system would support the firm's network-wide strategic, tactical, and operational planning activities. AO fully implemented its HMD planning framework in about two years, and Figure 6.3 depicts the completed system. This framework positioned AO to generate coordinated

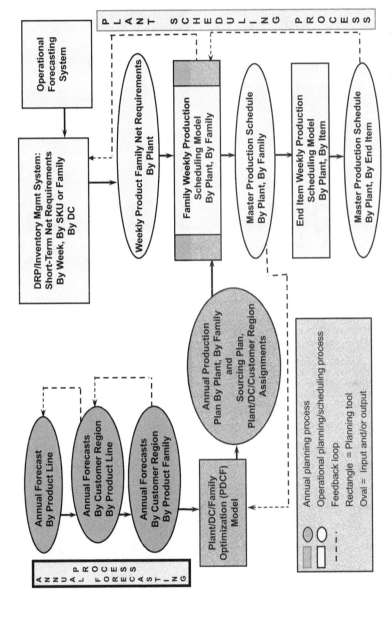

Figure 6.3 AO's hierarchical manufacturing and distribution planning framework (tactical/annual planning and operational scheduling)

strategic, tactical, and operational plans and schedules. We will now briefly review the components of this system, focusing first on tactical and operational planning and scheduling. We will then address how this framework also facilitated strategic planning.

Because annual and 18-month rolling planning horizons represent the most common tactical planning horizons, we illustrate an integrated annual and operational planning and scheduling system. Note that the dark shaded boxes and ovals in Figure 6.3 indicate elements of the annual planning process, while the other boxes and ovals constitute the operational planning and scheduling process.

Tactical (Annual) Planning Process

The process begins with the development of annual or 12- to 18-month rolling forecasts by major product lines. For this example, we assume a product hierarchy consisting, from top to bottom, of (1) major product line, (2) product family, and (3) end item, where product families represent aggregations of similar end items and product lines represent aggregations of similar product families. Techniques used to generate forecasts at this level vary widely and include econometric forecasting, exponential smoothing[5] time series-based forecasting methods, and so on. Importantly, exogenous market intelligence and sales judgment factors often provide critical inputs at this level. Thus, a firm's ability to structure a process that effectively integrates quantitative techniques and qualitative inputs represents a key determinant of the accuracy of major product line forecasts.

The next step consists of disaggregating national product line forecasts into product line forecasts by customer region. Methodologies for generating these lower-level product line forecasts again vary widely and range from simple techniques such as using recent historical ratios of each customer region's demand to total demand to complex quantitative approaches.[6] Next, customer region product line forecasts are disaggregated

---

[5]Exponential smoothing is a short-range forecasting technique that forecasts next period's demand using the current period's forecast adjusted by a portion of this period's forecasting error.

[6]See Gupta et al. (2002).

into product family forecasts by customer region. AO used the recent historical percentage that each product family comprised of a customer region's total sales to disaggregate a customer region product line forecast into individual product family forecasts.

The product family forecasts by customer regions are important inputs for tactical/annual planning, and specifically for the plant/distribution center/product family optimization model. Linear and mixed integer programming optimization[7] models are the standard analytic decision support tools utilized for planning at the tactical/annual level. Annual optimization models most frequently define products at the product family level.[8] Further, assuming that the HMD application involves multiple manufacturing or distribution locations, these annual optimization models define demand by geographic regions. Hence the need for annual product family forecasts by customer region. Figure 6.4 highlights some

---

- **Distribution plan**
  - Assigns sales regions to DC's and plants (i.e., a sourcing plan)
  - Establishes plant to DC and inter-DC shipping (supply) plans
- **Annual production plan, for each plant, by time period**
  - Establishes planned operating rates for each plant (i.e., capacity utilization rates)
  - Assigns production product mixes for each plant (by defined product families)
- **Inventory plan for planning horizon, by time period**

Figure 6.4 Outputs from optimization model

---

[7]Linear programming is a mathematical technique that either maximizes or minimizes a linear function (an objective function) subject to satisfying defined linear constraints. For example, a production scheduling problem to be solved by a linear programming model would typically have an objective function "to create a production schedule that minimizes production costs" subject to satisfying the forecast "demand" constraints and "production capacity" constraints defined for the problem. Mixed integer programming is a related mathematical technique that can solve more complicated problems such as whether or not to open or close facilities on a network (i.e., what are termed 0–1 type decisions).

[8]Hax and Meal (1975).

of the key outputs derived from the annual plant/DC/family (PDCF) optimization model. (Figure 6.3 also illustrates these outputs.)

As shown in Figure 6.3, the last major step of the annual planning process consists of evaluating the annual optimization model's production plans for each plant in a weekly production scheduling model. Briefly, this family weekly production scheduling model helps to determine whether the production plans developed for a plant by the annual model remain feasible when evaluated at a greater level of detail than possible in an annual model. Typical examples include evaluating production plans in weekly time buckets rather than in quarterly buckets or a single annual bucket and evaluating the impact of weekly production changeovers on the feasibility of an annual production plan. The weekly production scheduling model produces a master production schedule for a plant at the family level. It is not unusual to find that production plans that appeared feasible at the annual level manifest infeasibilities when evaluated at the weekly level. This occurs because annual integrated manufacturing/distribution models typically do not include changeover costs or setup times, nor do they define time buckets at weekly levels. Thus, in Figure 6.3, the feedback loop shown between the output of the weekly plant scheduling model and the annual optimization model represents a critical part of the annual planning process. Clearly, a firm must develop an annual production plan that each of its plants can feasibly implement at the operational level. The feedback loop from the weekly model to the annual model ensures this. (Chapter 8 will illustrate feedback loops in more detail.)

This completes the integrated annual hierarchical generic planning process. Next, we briefly review the operational planning and scheduling process. Based on the tactical (annual) planning process, as indicated in Figure 6.4, sourcing patterns have been defined (e.g., what plant serves which distribution center, and what distribution center serves which customer region). The operational planning and scheduling system executes these decisions on a day-to-day and week-to-week basis.

Operational Planning and Scheduling Process

Figure 6.3 illustrates a standard operational planning and scheduling system. A forecasting system, frequently time-series, exponential smoothing-based, generates forecasts at the item or stock keeping unit (SKU) level. These forecasts feed an inventory management system, often a DRP system, which generates net requirements by week, by SKU, and/or by family for each distribution center. The DCs place their weekly net requirements upon their source plants, and this creates the weekly net requirements by end item, by family for a manufacturing plant. These weekly net requirements drive the family weekly production scheduling model. Note that this short-run-focused scheduling model could be defined in different time buckets (e.g., days or 2-week periods) if appropriate. Also note that a feedback loop flows from the weekly scheduling model back to the inventory management module. Should the weekly scheduling model determine that a plant cannot meet the weekly family net requirements, this feedback loop communicates the infeasibilities. An iterative process would then ensue, whereby either the original net requirements are modified until a feasible plan can be produced or excess production requirements are addressed by such options as overtime production or the offloading of some net requirements to other plants.

The final major step outlined in the generic process of Figure 6.3 is the plant's master production schedule by end item. The plant's weekly master production schedule by family provides the input that drives the end item scheduling model. This model produces a traditional master production schedule of end items by weekly time buckets. Note that a feedback loop also flows from the master production end item schedule back to the weekly family production scheduling model. This feedback loop is required because it is possible that a schedule that appears feasible at the weekly, family level may mask infeasibilities that become evident at the end item level. This completes our discussion of the tactical and operational components of AO's HMD framework, illustrated in Figure 6.3.[9]

---

[9]The reader familiar with the S&OP (Sales and Operations Planning) Process may recognize that a number of the forecasting, inventory management, and capacity planning tools described in the AO Tile hierarchical planning system are also the types of tools often used by functions such as demand management, logistics, and manufacturing to develop inputs and outputs for a firm's monthly S&OP process. Although HMD planning frameworks and systems are not typically developed just to support an S&OP process, the components of these frameworks can often be leveraged for multiple purposes, including S&OP support.

The implementation of this framework and system reduced the firm's annual operating costs by about 10 percent. Additionally, it facilitated fully integrated tactical and short-run production and distribution plans and schedules, resulting in enhanced customer service levels and significantly reduced "unplanned" emergency interfacility inventory transfers.[10]

As described, this system is generic in that it is applicable to a wide range of industries and firms. Individual firms may use a subset or perhaps variations on all the framework components reviewed. Some firms will have additional components not covered here. Regardless of the particular components employed by an individual firm, the key requirement remains that all of the modules of an HMD system must be linked together in a coordinated, hierarchical approach, as AO's system illustrates.

We close this section by noting that for many firms, including AO, there exist many critical operational planning and scheduling activities that occur after (and are often driven by) end item schedules. Systems that generate schedules for components of the end item represent just one example. We will not attempt to address these activities, but rather simply recognize that many of these work-in-process and raw materials plans and schedules have hierarchical characteristics like those reviewed at the finished goods level.

Strategic Planning Support

The tactical and operational planning system of AO also supported the firm's strategic planning process. To understand how, consider Figure 6.3 and the following example. The tactical PDCF optimization model contained the following data:

- The production costs, rates, capacities, and product mix capabilities of each production line at each plant, by product family
- The distribution center costs, rates and capacities at each DC on AO's network, by product family

---

[10]See Miller (2002).

- The freight and related costs to transport product between each plant and each DC, and between each DC and each customer region on the network
- The forecast demand by product family for each customer region

AO's standard tactical business planning process required that its planning team update all the inputs to the PDCF model at least once every six months. The standardization of this business process assured that the firm always had current data available on all the key manufacturing and distribution costs, rates, and capacities for its network. For strategic planning purposes, this represented an extremely important capability. For example, over time, it became clear that AO's distribution center storage and throughput capacity would have to expand to meet the firm's increasing demand. The availability and currency of the PDCF model and other tactical decision support components such as the forecasting models positioned AO to rapidly generate powerful quantitative assessments of its network expansion options. Specifically, to support its strategic planning process, AO could easily modify its existing tactical PDCF models to include potential new DC or plant locations to add to its network. This, of course, required that the firm develop estimates of the costs and capacities of potential new facilities. AO would then evaluate through its optimization models how each potential new location would impact the entire network and what new location to pursue. Therefore, because AO updated its tactical planning tools regularly, it could readily engage in strategic planning assessments of its network at any time with relatively minimal notice.

Summary

This business process gave the firm a truly agile hierarchical planning capability. In addition to its standard operational and tactical planning process, it could launch into a strategic planning exercise very rapidly at any time should this be required. Additionally, the firm conducted a regularly scheduled strategic planning process annually. If AO had not devoted the time and resources necessary to maintain its robust tactical and operational planning framework and decision support tools, its strategic planning process would have similarly deteriorated. Finally, it is also important to recognize that the linkages between AO's strategic, tactical, and operational planning processes, facilitated by a well-defined hierarchical framework, ensured aligned decision making in the manufacturing and distribution functions from top to bottom.

Promoting the Use of Optimization and Related DSS Methods

The hierarchical logistics network planning framework presented earlier in this chapter utilized a variety of analytics tools (see Figure 6.3). Later, we will review other optimization, simulation, and related decision support system (DSS) logistics applications. Before delving into more models, however, let's first consider a well-tested managerial approach for facilitating the development and implementation of these types of tools. The following approach is particularly recommended when an organization has multiple key decision support gaps that managers believe must be filled.

On the basis of implementations in a number of industries, including pharmaceutical, consumer healthcare, consumer packaged goods, and ceramic tile, the authors have employed a specific strategy to promote the use of analytics-based DSS techniques within a firm's operations. The following steps outline this strategy from the perspective of a manager seeking to develop and implement effective tools such as optimization or simulation for his or her operation.

1. Evaluate your operation from the hierarchical, multiple planning period perspective previously described.
2. Select the planning activity or function within your overall operation that can benefit most immediately from the introduction of analytics-based decision support techniques. The factors that dictate this decision will vary by firm. Decision factors would include what facet of one's operation has the greatest need for enhanced DSS support, what project has the greatest likelihood of success, and what project has the highest probability of stimulating further DSS enhancements.

3. Staff the project with a colleague or colleagues who are employees of the firm and, ideally, who are already established within the operation where the implementation will occur (i.e., do not rely solely on third-party consultants to develop the DSS for your operation.)

4. Utilize consultants to assist on the project only if necessary (e.g., if the skill sets and/or resources are not fully available internally). However, an internal employee must lead the project. Additionally, there must be one or more internal employees with the skill sets and knowledge to develop, implement, and effectively utilize optimization, simulation, and related decision support tools. If there are internal resources who have the skill sets to utilize the applications, this will ensure continuity once the firm implements the planning methodology.

5. Establish the use of this DSS tool as a standard business practice, once the initial DSS application is developed. The frequency with which the firm's operation will utilize the DSS tool will naturally vary depending on the application. However, the critical point is that the role of this DSS tool in the operation's planning and scheduling activities be well defined.

6. Utilize the initial DSS applications to create a foundation from which to build and append additional related DSS planning tools and methodologies for the organization.

The strategy outlined in steps one to six sketches some basic high-level steps that have led to the successful implementations of DSS applications and hierarchical planning frameworks. Clearly, there exist many more detailed steps necessary to facilitate a successful project. However, these six steps provide a general overview of the recommended approach.

Once the DSS application has been developed and the initial implementation occurs, steps five and six assume critical importance. The manager(s) responsible for the DSS must ensure that the analytics methods become an integral, standard component of the planning activity the DSS supports. Thus, the key question becomes how to ensure this progression. Steps three and four provide the answer.

Step three indicates that to manage the project one must select employees who have existing roles and responsibilities within the firm. Having one or more key internal employees lead the development and implementation of the DSS project ensures that there will be an in-house "advocate or champion" of the DSS on an ongoing basis. For this reason, if the sponsoring manager of the project can appoint two or more employees to major roles in the DSS project, this further enhances the ongoing support and advocacy for the system. Additionally, employees who hold key or central positions in the operation where the DSS will be implemented represent the best candidates to lead the DSS project—again because this will facilitate a very strong ongoing advocacy for the system. Similarly, should a sponsoring manager find it necessary to employ consultants to staff significant portions of the DSS project, it becomes important that the sponsor have a good exit strategy for the consultant(s). Specifically, an effective transition process must take place whereby internal employees must quickly assume ongoing operational responsibility for any portions of the system developed by the consultant(s). If this "hand-off" does not occur quickly, there is a significantly greater probability that the DSS will not become ingrained into the firm's operation. Instead, the new system risks ending up unused "on the shelf" because it lacks ongoing supporters within the firm's operations.

With the appropriate advocacy established in steps three and four, we return to steps five and six. As noted, in step five the sponsoring manager must establish the use of an analytics-based DSS as a standard business practice. Depending on the level in the hierarchical planning framework (Figure 6.3) that the DSS supports, the operation may employ the tool as frequently as daily or as infrequently as quarterly to annually. Regardless of the appropriate frequency, the sponsoring manager and project advocates (i.e., the key employees who led the development project) must take the necessary steps to facilitate the DSS integration. This may represent a very simple or significant undertaking depending on the situation. If the project "advocates" plan to utilize the DSS in their own planning activities and area of responsibility, integrating the DSS as a standard business practice requires simply that these managers execute an implementation plan. Once implemented, the DSS becomes a core or standard business practice. However, if the sponsoring manager and DSS advocates must influence others to utilize the DSS to support planning activities that are either not their (the advocates') direct responsibility or are relatively remote (e.g., in distant plants), step five becomes far more difficult. For this reason, we highly recommend that in the initial DSS project selection process, the sponsoring manager choose an application that will support his or her area of responsibility directly. Further, we recommend that the manager select a DSS project that will support an operation or planning activity with which the manager has regular and direct contact. This will again facilitate a successful integration of the DSS as a standard business practice.

We now consider step six, where the initial DSS implementation project becomes the foundation tool that stimulates the growth of an expanded system over time. Based on the implementations previously cited in this book, as well as other successful implementations, the authors have observed a consistent pattern: A successful DSS implementation will "eventually" support several activities or operations in addition to the initial application. Several factors contribute to this.

An optimization project or similar large-scale DSS effort requires numerous data inputs. These data inputs can often support secondary DSS applications not originally envisioned when the initial system was planned. For example, the developers of the DSS reported in Gupta et al. (2002) originally constructed this system to provide general support for DC operations and customer logistics scorecards. However, when the operation that this DSS supported suddenly had significant storage capacity issues in the early to mid- 2000s, the developers rapidly created another DSS to provide daily inventory deployment guidance for the over capacitated network (see the "Warehouse Operations Decision Support" section in this chapter). In developing this second DSS, the in-house team relied heavily on the data sets and existing data interfaces that supported the initial DSS. In some cases, the team simply augmented an existing interface from the firm's Enterprise Resource Planning system (ERP) to the existing DSS with additional data fields. These additional fields appended to the existing interface facilitated the rapid development of algorithms that formed the basis of a daily inventory deployment DSS. In this example, the fact that the firm already had one successful DSS in place—a "foundation"— paved the way for the rapid implementation of a second DSS.

A similar evolution occurred at AO. As described earlier in this chapter, this firm developed and implemented a mathematical optimization model that generated integrated tactical manufacturing and distribution plans (i.e., the PDCF model in Figure 6.3). This DSS model quickly became a key component of the firm's standard tactical planning business process. This optimization model became the "foundation" tool that then spawned the development of several related DSS implementations at this firm over the next several years. In this case, the original optimization model generated very significant savings, as well as customer service level improvements for the firm. The success of this initial implementation created great interest at AO in further improving the quality of key data inputs to this model. In particular, the firm next developed a new tactical forecasting system to provide product family demand projections to the integrated manufacturing and distribution model. This integrated top-down/bottom-up forecasting system replaced a previous manual, anecdotal, and judgment-based forecasting approach, and it dramatically improved the firm's forecast accuracy. Next, as the firm scrutinized its new optimization-based manufacturing and distribution planning system, it realized that it needed to improve the start of period inventory data inputs to its planning process. Specifically, the firm discerned that its aggregated inventory inputs to the production planning process were leading to production schedules that created poor customer service line item fill rates. Briefly, the aggregated inventory inputs did not properly recognize serious inventory imbalances that could exist at the end item and product family level. To correct this problem, the firm developed a DSS that evaluated its inventory simultaneously at multiple levels (i.e., at the end item and product family levels). This DSS application became a preprocessing step that the firm utilized to develop its inventory inputs to the tactical production planning process.

The examples cited in this section illustrate how an initial DSS implementation stimulates the development of additional DSS applications over time. As noted, a well-implemented DSS typically provides secondary and tertiary benefits and decision support for additional problems beyond those that the developers of such systems explicitly designed in the original application. Additionally, once an initial optimization model or similar analytics method enables the DSS to provide significant contributions to a firm, this usually spawns further interest and inquiries from other managers in an organization. Specifically, managers who observe a

DSS system improving the effectiveness of decision making in another function in their firm become interested in utilizing similar methodologies to support their own areas of functional responsibility. This can lead to either new DSS projects or the expansion of existing DSS implementations. In either case, a key point remains that the original DSS project creates a foundation from which to build other applications to benefit a firm. This further illustrates the importance for a manager of carefully identifying and implementing an initial DSS project.

Lessons Learned and Final Thoughts

The hierarchical planning framework reviewed at the outset of this chapter provides a unifying perspective with which to view existing and potential DSS applications in a firm. An organization with strong capabilities will have DSS systems to support planning activities at the strategic, tactical, and operational levels (i.e., support for all planning horizons). For the manager of a firm seeking to enhance internal logistics DSS capabilities, a review of the firm's current DSS across all planning horizons represents a good starting point. This review will serve to identify those planning activities that could benefit the most from additional support.

Once the sponsoring manager has selected a DSS application for development and implementation, it is critical to keep in mind that optimization and similar analytics-based techniques remain unknown, "black box" methods for many firms and managers. Thus, the success of a DSS application may hinge on whether the sponsoring manager can install one or more internal project leads who have strong operational knowledge, leadership and communications skills, as well as a good comfort level with technical analytics methodologies. Finally, once the DSS application is developed and implemented, the sponsoring manager must quickly incorporate this new capability into the firm's standard business planning process.

In summary, there is no one "right way" to implement optimization and other DSS techniques into a firm's core planning processes. However, the approaches outlined in this section have facilitated a number of successful implementations in different firms and industries. It is hoped that the approaches described herein may offer some useful insights for other potential applications.

Integrating Warehouse Design and Strategic Logistics Network Planning

An earlier section in this chapter described a general framework for integrated manufacturing and distribution network planning and operations. In this section, we now briefly illustrate how a firm can incorporate key decisions such as the internal design of warehouses (DCs) into this integrative logistics network planning approach.[11]

The typical strategic logistics network design problem considers variables such as the number of warehouses required, customer service delivery requirements, the inventory investment required under alternative network configurations, inbound and outbound freight costs, and facility (i.e., warehouse) costs. Facility costs include factors such as labor, land, construction, taxes, and other regional location variables.

Developing the optimal network design strategy and configuration requires that a firm evaluate appropriate trade-offs between all pertinent cost and service variables. For example, the number and location of warehouses on a network (e.g., a domestic US network) will impact the cost of inbound freight versus outbound freight. Typically, a network with many warehouses will have lower outbound customer delivery freight costs than will a network with one or a few warehouses. On the other hand, inbound freight costs from plants and other supply points to warehouses (DCs) may be higher on a network with many customer-facing DCs than on a network with one or two DCs located in close proximity to the major supply points. A good network study and strategy must examine these and all other trade-offs.

One key trade-off in logistics network studies and strategies that frequently does not receive enough scrutiny concerns the level of technology and automation planned in warehouse operations. The authors' experience over several decades in logistics management suggests that too frequently firms approach a logistics study with either a "predetermined"

---

[11]Some of the concepts and text in this section previously appeared in *Materials Handling and Logistics Magazine* (February 2011), and are presented here with the kind permission of MH&L.

view of the type of warehouse to be employed on the network or, alternatively, just a general concept of the capacity planned for a new warehouse based on a previously completed network study.

The Predetermined and the Post-Network Study Approaches

The size of existing distribution centers and the technologies used in existing centers often shape a "predetermined" view. Alternatively, some firms design their optimal "four walls" warehouse layout and technology in isolation after first evaluating their distribution network (e.g., after determining the location and required capacity of a new warehouse). These approaches result in firms treating the "network design" strategy and the "warehouse four walls design strategy" as two separate problems rather than as one integrated problem and strategy.

Typical planning sequences that too often unfold are as follows. In the "predetermined" case, logistics planners first determine the basic facility layout, capacity, and technology that represent their "standard" configuration for each DC on their network—i.e., a basic template or model for their DCs. Naturally, some variations in facility size and other variables will be allowed. However, the firm will establish a basic design and technology configuration for DCs on the firm's network. With this determination complete, logistics planners then turn their attention to the optimal number and locations of warehouses for their network. In this second stage of the network design problem, the firm then conducts the standard trade-off analyses between freight costs, warehouse location costs (e.g., taxes, land, and labor costs), FGI investment and carrying costs (as a function of the number of locations), target service levels, and so on.

Alternatively, when a firm designs its warehouse(s) after conducting its logistics network study, the opposite sequence occurs. First, the firm performs its evaluation of freight, warehouse location, and other logistics costs, and after this step the warehouse layout, technology, and automation planning take place.

In either case, this two-stage, nonintegrated network design approach can result in a suboptimal overall network strategy. This will occur because the cost, productivity and capacity implications that alternative warehouse technologies may offer are not integrated into the logistics network analysis. What is required instead is that the one-time investment costs associated with different levels and types of technologies employed in a warehouse, and the differences in productivity levels and annual operating costs associated with different technologies and levels of automation, must be explicitly integrated into the network design stage. Only a fully integrated analytics methodology can correctly evaluate all the trade-offs and identify the optimal level of warehouse technology and automation for a logistics network, as well as the optimal number of locations, capacities, and service levels.

The Optimal Strategic Logistics Network Planning Approach

To ensure an optimal network design and warehouse strategy requires an iterative, integrated approach to the planning process. The following illustrates this method, which the authors recommend. For this illustration, we assume that a firm is just initiating a logistics network study. The study team consists of two subteams: (a) a network design team and (b) a warehouse design team. The planning process proceeds as follows:

1. The network design team performs an initial evaluation of warehouse locations and warehouse roles on the basis of traditional factors previously cited. A logistics network optimization model typically supports this evaluation process.
2. Concurrently, the warehouse design team explores a range of warehouse layouts, technologies, and capacities. Factors such as the type and configuration of storage systems versus labor requirements, height of storage systems versus warehouse floor space required, type of manually supported material handling equipment (e.g., forklifts) versus more automated storage solutions, and manual versus automated picking and conveyance systems are evaluated.
3. The network design team then incorporates the warehouse design team's results as inputs to a second round of network design evaluations. In this second round, the network design team simultaneously considers both potential warehouse locations and potential alternative warehouse designs and capacities. For example, multiple types of warehouses (more manual versus more automated) with multiple

storage and picking capacity levels may be evaluated for one potential location in this phase. Additionally, scenarios with different numbers of warehouses and different technologies will receive consideration.

4. The evaluation continues with as many iterations as required between the warehouse design team and the network design team until the teams identify the optimal, aligned network and warehouse designs.

Full Integration

In a fully integrated logistics network analysis, the opportunity to create a strategic advantage through improved service and reduced cost is much more likely, as the exogenous variables, such as labor rates, utility rates, taxes, and freight costs, are balanced with the opportunity to use technology to control factors such as the amount of labor and utilities required within the warehouse. This approach facilitates a holistic view and balancing of total logistic network annual operating costs, investment costs, and service levels. The integrated evaluation of all these variables facilitates solutions that can provide a strategic advantage for a firm and value for its customers.

Warehouse Operations Decision Support

Once a firm has successfully implemented a logistics planning framework and accompanying analytics-based tools, it can respond rapidly and effectively to unexpected operating challenges. In this section, we present a case study that illustrates how a strong DSS facilitates: (1) agile logistics operations, and (2) the rapid development of additional new DSS components when needed to address sudden operational challenges.

In the early 2000s, following the merger of WL and Pfizer, significant storage capacity pressures suddenly began to impact the warehouse operations of the consumer distribution network. Specifically, the total pallets of FGI of the newly merged consumer division of Pfizer substantially exceeded the in-house pallet storage capacity of the consumer distribution network. The merger and several unanticipated internal issues created this rapid inventory buildup and capacity deficit. Both WL and old Pfizer had previously used third-party overflow warehouse storage on an occasional, seasonal basis in the past. However, by 2001, it became clear that the newly merged firm would have to employ third-party warehouse storage space as a standard component of its everyday operating storage capacity. Neither a significant investment in internal storage capacity nor opening a new third-party full-service, customer-facing DC represented acceptable options. Thus, Pfizer Logistics had to address its infrastructure capacity deficit with third-party overflow warehouse storage. Further, it had to formulate and implement an operating plan rapidly to contain this quickly developing threat to service levels. The combination of warehouse congestion and difficulties deploying the right inventory to the correct warehouse locations (given all the excess inventory) threatened to escalate into a serious issue. Throughput capacity, unlike storage capacity, did not represent an issue because the consumer DCs had ample throughput capacity.

To understand the potential complexity of managing the Pfizer consumer network with at times over 50 percent of FGI in outside overflow storage, consider Figure 6.5. This figure depicts the numerous different flows of finished goods into and out of the firm's two customer-facing distribution centers. As Figure 6.5 illustrates, finished goods produced at Pfizer plants and contract-manufacturing locations could potentially flow to copackers, to third-party outside storage locations, or directly to the Pfizer DCs, depending upon inventory requirements at any particular time. (Copackers are third-party vendors who operate manual kitting operations that transform base finished goods products into promotional display items commonly found at grocery, drug, mass merchandiser, and other retail outlets.[12])

Inbound shipments to the Pfizer DCs could originate from Pfizer plants, Pfizer contract manufacturers, copackers, and third-party outside storage locations. In total, inbound shipments to the DCs originated from well over 40 different locations. Finally, as Figure 6.5 depicts, the Pfizer DCs themselves often had to ship finished goods to copackers and to outside storage locations in addition to the DCs' shipments outbound to customers.

This potentially complex set of product flows is characteristic of consumer firms and industries. Thus, many manufacturers have a strong need

---

[12]Besides display pallets, copackers create promotional finished goods such as "on-packs." An on-pack is a promotional item where one finished good unit (e.g., a unit of toothpaste) is attached to another finished good unit (e.g., a bottle of Listerine) to create a new promotional unit.

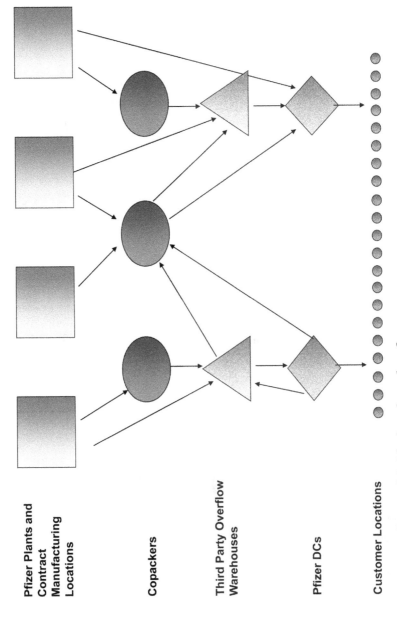

Pfizer Plants and Contract Manufacturing Locations

Copackers

Third Party Overflow Warehouses

Pfizer DCs

Customer Locations

Figure 6.5 Potential finished goods product flows

for DSS that can guide daily deployment operations that are more complex than the traditional "plant to manufacturer's DC to retailer's DC" flow. While traditional DSS tools such as DRP systems can effectively provide decision support for the regular replenishment flows (e.g., of open stock base items), firms that manage the complex consumer products flows described herein often require additional DSS guidance.

To manage its complex set of product flows and inventory positioning decisions, Pfizer Logistics determined that it required an analytics-based DSS that would facilitate the effective daily deployment of inventory between all locations. This included daily inventory flows from:

- Outside storage locations to the DCs
- Plants, copackers, and contract-manufacturing locations to the DCs
- Plants, copackers, and contract-manufacturing locations to outside storage locations, and
- DCs to outside storage locations and copackers

The firm's ERP and warehouse management systems (WMS), although quite advanced, did not have sophisticated capabilities to deploy inventory between outside and inside storage locations. Thus, Pfizer Logistics decided that it would have to construct a DSS to provide the functionality just described.

DSS Development Approach

Pfizer Logistics had already developed and implemented an extensive DSS similar to the logistics framework and components described earlier in this chapter in the "Strategic, Tactical, and Operational Manufacturing and Distribution Network Modeling" section. Now to create a new operational DSS to guide daily decision making on inventory deployment and warehouse operations, the logistics group leveraged the underlying data of this previously constructed DSS. An informal team consisting of operations colleagues from the DCs and several colleagues from headquarters with business analytics and operations research backgrounds was formed. The team rapidly developed specifications for a series of daily reports that would help warehouse operations direct inventory deployment operations each morning. Specifically, the DSS had to provide guidance on all potential inventory deployment flows between all locations. This included all inventory item-level flows involving plants, contract-manufacturing locations, copackers, overflow warehouses, and the Pfizer DCs — a very extensive set of potential moves.

Data Flows to Support DSS

To support its existing DSS, the logistics group had previously established processes and the necessary interfaces to facilitate nightly flows of files, including the following data sets from corporate IT systems:

1. The current inventory positions of all items at all locations,
2. All orders for all items at all locations for as far into the future as they existed,
3. All forecasts for all items at all locations for as far into the future as they existed, and
4. Shipment (i.e., sales) history for all locations for all items for the most recent 12 months.

These files and data sets, providing up-to-date information as of the close of business from the previous day, were received by a local server at the logistics headquarters and used to update a local logistics server and data warehouse. The logistics team determined what additional data fields it needed besides those already received in nightly flows from corporate IT. Because data feeds supporting the existing logistics DSS were already in place, it became a quick, easy task to append additional fields to these nightly flows, once logistics identified the newly required fields. Colleagues in the logistics group configured the new DSS to automatically run a series of decision support analyses and reports each morning based on the updated data available on the logistics server.

The full set of morning reports collectively prioritized the unloading of inbound trucks at the DCs, directed the flow of newly produced FGI to either the DCs or their outside storage locations, and directed the flows of inventory between the outside storage locations of the DCs and the DCs themselves. Figure 6.6 offers an overview of the primary data flows

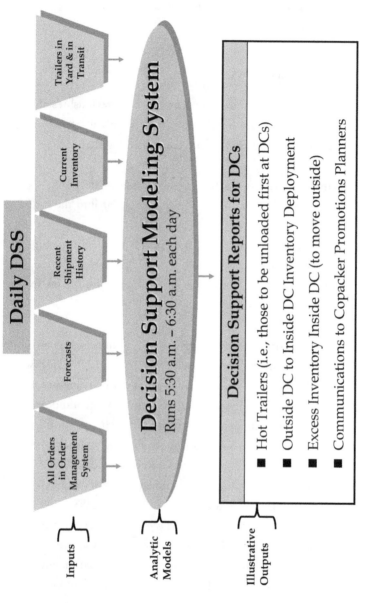

Inputs

Daily DSS

All Orders in Order Management System

Forecasts

Recent Shipment History

Current Inventory

Trailers in Yard & in Transit

Analytic Models

Decision Support Modeling System
Runs 5:30 a.m. – 6:30 a.m. each day

Illustrative Outputs

Decision Support Reports for DCs

■ Hot Trailers (i.e., those to be unloaded first at DCs)

■ Outside DC to Inside DC Inventory Deployment

■ Excess Inventory Inside DC (to move outside)

■ Communications to Copacker Promotions Planners

Figure 6.6 Methodology and algorithms of DSS

and basic methodology of the system. The DSS received complete data updates every night from each key component of the customer order fulfillment IT infrastructure, namely, the order management system (of the ERP), the warehouse and trailer yard management system, and the transportation scheduling system. These nightly data flows updated the DSS with the most current inventory positions of all items at all locations, all orders, and forecasts for all items at all locations; shipment history for all items at all locations; and in-transit and in-yard trailer information providing inventory information for all items on all trailers.

Summary

The Pfizer Logistics organization implemented the initial version of this DSS very rapidly, and the team began to use individual analyses as soon as the first version of a planning analysis/report was constructed. A process quickly evolved whereby the team modified and enhanced individual analyses daily. The colleagues in warehouse operations would employ the updated DSS component for a day or two and then request additional modifications based on learnings from using the DSS. Over time, each individual analysis of the DSS provided better, more precise day-to-day operational guidance. Similarly, the presentation formats of the analyses improved over time and offered clearer, easier-to-understand guidance for the logistics organization. Finally, often over several weeks or months, individual DSS components reached their final analytic and presentation formats. Within approximately 2 to 3 months, the team had designed, developed, tested, and implemented the first full set of core algorithms and analyses. These initial core algorithms provided enough guidance to facilitate the effective use of overflow outside storage. Over the next year or so after the initial implementation, refinements and enhancements to this DSS tool continued, and it was used for many years thereafter.

The rapid implementation of the inventory deployment system produced many short- and longer-term benefits. The daily inventory deployment decision support of this system prevented an estimated $20 million of potential annual revenue losses and allowed Pfizer to maintain a high level of customer service. The ongoing commitment of the logistics organization to flexible, agile DSS capabilities allowed it to respond quickly and effectively to a situation that could have significantly damaged its customer service levels.[13]

Conclusion

The case studies and frameworks presented in this chapter illustrate the need for a firm's manufacturing and distribution organizations to provide decision support at all levels of the planning hierarchy: the strategic, tactical, and operational levels. DSS cannot be shortchanged. The manufacturing and distribution organizations must arm their colleagues with the data and analytics tools required to make good decisions and plans. Managers must also ensure that they have personnel who have the skill sets to exploit good DSS.

---

[13]Readers interested in additional details on the algorithms developed, the analyses created, and the reporting formats are referred to Miller et al. (2013).

CHAPTER 7

Inventory Management
Decision Support

Introduction

Inventory planning and management represents a critical component of logistics management. Insufficient levels and/or poor positioning and deployment practices can severely damage customer service fill rates. Conversely, prolonged excess inventory levels can damage a firm's financial performance and also create operational inefficiencies (e.g., overcrowded, underperforming warehouse operations). Thus, integrating inventory planning with overall logistics network planning activities is critical.

In this chapter, we illustrate an approach that facilitates determining an integrated network/facility design and inventory investment/deployment plan. Recall that Chapter 6 previously described a decision support methodology to integrate network design and internal warehouse facility "four walls" design. Now, we extend this discussion by explicitly incorporating inventory planning into this integrative process. In the following section, we illustrate how this approach differs from the practice one often observes in industry where many firms conduct their long-run inventory and network/facility design activities separately. Specifically, we present a framework and methodology for integrating network, facility, and inventory planning. Then, in a later section in this chapter, we turn to the operational level of inventory management, illustrating a simple yet effective inventory analytics and reporting system to monitor firm inventory levels.

Case Study: An Integrated Inventory, Facility, and Network Design Planning Approach

To integrate inventory planning explicitly into strategic and tactical logistics network design planning requires several additional inputs and models to complement those already discussed in Chapter 6. For illustrative purposes, we consider a case study of a firm, Pfizer, that projected its logistics network infrastructure requirements, by year, five years into the future. The interest and need for this DSS first arose during the warehouse storage capacity challenges the firm encountered in the early 2000s (see Chapter 6). This unpredicted storage capacity crunch materialized quickly and, as noted, with little warning, prompting the question of how long this situation would last. Thus, while the operational guidance generated by the DSS discussed in Chapter 6 facilitated effective short-term customer service saving actions, Pfizer also responded by developing the strategic DSS displayed in Figure 7.1.

This DSS combined several existing DSS components (e.g., the Distribution Network Optimization Model), with new analytics tools to create an integrated network facility and inventory planning DSS. Once implemented, this planning methodology became a standard, core business logistics process conducted at least once a year.

Inventory Planning Models

The inventory investment model shown in Figure 7.1 represented a major planning element in Pfizer Logistics' strategic DSS. Several inventory

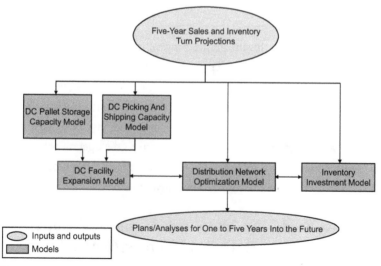

Figure 7.1 **Strategic and tactical network planning components**

models were constructed over the years, including a traditional item-level statistical safety stock model and several high-level "portfolio effect" and "square root of N" models.[14] For most strategic applications, the portfolio effect and square root of N models provided sufficient accuracy. Additionally, Pfizer's ERP system provided safety stock targets to meet desired fill rates for all end items and, in total, at each of the firm's DCs. Thus, between the ERP-based inventory management requirements for its existing network and the DSS inventory investment model, Pfizer Logistics could project finished goods investment requirements both for its existing DCs and for any alternative potential DC network it wished to evaluate.

An Illustrative Network Capacity Planning Scenario

To support long-run warehouse network capacity planning, Pfizer developed three "linked" simulation models: (1) a DC storage capacity model, (2) a DC picking and shipping model, and (3) a DC facility expansion model (see Figure 7.1). The DC storage capacity and DC picking and shipping models were often jointly referred to as the "workload models" because they simulated anticipated workloads. These three models or submodels collectively served to evaluate the capacity requirements and projections for the DCs on Pfizer's network over planning horizons that ranged typically between two and five years depending on the decision in question. For illustrative purposes, we now review a typical strategic planning exercise that Pfizer conducted using the decision support models displayed in Figure 7.1. This exercise required that Pfizer determine whether its warehouse network had sufficient capacity to address its projected demands for the next five years.

A sales forecast from marketing for the five-year strategic planning horizon drove the warehouse capacity planning exercise. Often a "sales forecast" really consisted of a series of alternative forecast scenarios, each with a projected probability of occurring. These alternative forecasts facilitated sensitivity analyses on the "base case" (or most likely forecast scenario).

---

[14]For background on these models, see e.g., Maister (1976); Evers and Beier (1993); Tyagi and Das (1998); and Miller et al. (2016)

Next, estimates of FGI requirements were developed for the current network and any alternative network scenarios using the ERP inventory management module and the inventory investment model. Specifically, Pfizer logistics employed a combination of the firm's five-year inventory turns' targets and inventory investment model simulations to generate projected FGI requirements by year. Additionally, high and low inventory turns scenarios, in addition to the firm's turns target goals, were modeled.

Subsequently, planners input the sales and inventory projections for the planning horizon into the DC storage capacity and the DC picking and shipping capacity models. These models simulated storage and picking requirements by week over the five-year horizon so that they could generate maximum and minimum requirements projections, as well as averages, for each year. Thus, these two DC workload submodels each projected the capacity utilization rates (surplus or deficit) over the entire planning horizon for their respective areas of warehouse operations by week. The outputs of these two submodels became inputs to the DC facility expansion model. The DC facility expansion model evaluated such factors as the total network-wide warehouse square footage required to store, pick, and ship the projected sales and inventory over the planning horizon. Figures 7.2 and 7.3 illustrate several representative inputs and outputs of these models.

As depicted in Figure 7.1, sales projections were also input into a network optimization planning model during the warehouse capacity evaluation process. Pfizer developed this optimization model of its US network during the first long-run warehouse planning evaluation that the strategic and tactical DSS was developed to support. The optimization model was a mixed integer programming model that provided distribution sourcing and supply plans for the planning horizon.[15] Results developed by this

---

[15]As described in the discussion of AO in Chapter 6, a network planning optimization model can be used to develop integrated tactical and strategic manufacturing and distribution plans for all plants and DCs on a firm's network. Alternatively, if manufacturing product sources and output levels are determined prior to the creation of detailed distribution plans, the network planning optimization model can provide the distribution plan for all flows across the network. In the Pfizer planning process (unlike the AO process), the manufacturing sources were determined prior to the development of the detailed distribution plan.

INPUT	FACTOR
1. Maximum throughput capacity of DC (annual cases above this require more facility sq. ft.)	40,000,000
2. Projected increase in cases above current max capacity—(note: input from throughput model)	15,000,000
3. Projected increase in storage pallets above current capacity—(note: input from storage model)	20,000
4. Increase in facility square feet required per increase of 1,000 cases of annual throughput (excluding inbound and staging space)	10
5. Increase in inbound and outbound staging sq. ft. required per increase of 1,000 cases of annual throughput	12
6. Increase in facility sq. ft. required per increase of 10 pallets in average inventory	40
7. Ratio of increase in racking positions required to increase in pallet storage locations required i.e., (racking positions)/(pallet storage locations)	1.25
8. Cost of storage rack per pallet position	50
9. Construction cost per sq. ft. of expansion at facility	65
10. Sq. ft. of land required per sq. ft. of facility expansion	2
11. Cost per sq. ft. of land purchased for expansion	20
12. Total sq. ft. of land available at facility	200,000
13. Additional supervisors to support full 2nd shift	5
14. Additional warehouse labor and other nonsupervisory personnel to support full 2nd shift	75
15. Cost of additional guard service and trailer yard spotter to support 2nd shift	120,000
16. Avg. annual cost of supervisor (salary + benefits)	110,000
17. Avg. annual cost of warehouse labor and nonsupervisory labor (salary + benefits)	70,000
18. One warehouse colleague must be added for every XX cases of annual throughput (above 2nd shift requirements)	250,000
19. One warehouse supervisor must be added for every XX additional warehouse labor colleagues (above 2nd shift requirements)	20
20. Number of material handling equipment units required to support full 2nd shift at facility	10
21. Avg. cost per material handling equipment unit purchased to support 2nd shift	30,000
22. Material handling units required to support expanded facility above requirements for 2nd shift	45
23. Avg. cost per material handling unit purchased to support expansion of facility above requirements for 2nd shift	30,000
24. Percentage increase (from current) in non-labor and non-material handling equipment costs for a full 2nd shift	25%
25. One-time costs to upgrade computer capacities associated with a full 2nd shift	100,000
26. One-time costs to upgrade computer capacity associated with capacity expansion above requirements for 2nd shift	100,000
27. Years to depreciate all machinery and equipment	10
28. Years to depreciate all building improvements costs	25
• Input values are illustrative and do not reflect actual costs or rates • The facility expansion model for each DC contained many other inputs not shown here	

Figure 7.2 Illustrative inputs to the warehouse facility expansion model

Output	Projection $(millions)
1. Total one-time cost to purchase and install racking	1.5
2. Total one-time cost for facility expansion construction	15.0
3. Total one-time cost to purchase land for expansion	1.0
4. Total one-time cost to purchase material handling equipment for 2nd shift	0.4
5. Total one-time cost to purchase material handling equipment to support expanded facility above requirements for 2nd shift	1.1
6. Total cost of additional labor for full 2nd shift	2.0
7. Total cost of additional labor to support facility above requirements for full 2nd shift	1.0
8. Total one-time cost of operating a 2nd shift and expanding facility	19.0
9. Total annual operating cost increase (excl. depreciation) associated with a full 2nd shift and expanding facility	3.0
10. Annual depreciation of capital costs required to support a full 2nd shift and expansion of the facility	1.3
11. Total annual operating cost increase (incl. depreciation) associated with a full 2nd shift and expanding facility	4.3
*Illustrative fictitious results for one warehouse in a scenario where both expanding a second shift and expanding the total facility were under consideration	

Figure 7.3 Illustrative outputs from the warehouse facility expansion model

model projected product flows through the network by individual location, from plants to customers. Thus, this model served to forecast the future product volumes that each warehouse would have to handle. In some applications, planners would run this model first before running the DC workload models so that the projected portion of total demand that each DC had responsibility for was clearly identified. In other cases, an existing supply and distribution plan was in place, and planners would input the initial planning horizon forecast directly into the DC workload models. In either case, an iterative planning process would ensue whereby the implications of results from the DC workload and facility expansion models would be evaluated in the network optimization model and vice versa. For example, if results from the DC workload model projected significant capacity shortages in three years, this would precipitate network optimization modeling exercises to explore expansion options (e.g., locating potential new DCs).

Finally, with respect to the network optimization model, it is important to point out that planners would also run optimization model scenarios that simultaneously considered freight, variable and fixed warehousing costs, warehouse storage and throughput capacity constraints, and so on (i.e., a more traditional optimization-based cost minimization approach). These types of modeling runs also included customer order cycle time constraints that were modeled by creating explicit transit time constraints (e.g., a constraint specifying that all customer locations must be served by a DC within three days' transit time of the customer location when served by motor carriers). For evaluative purposes, Pfizer Logistics found that an iterative and/or sequential modeling approach, supplemented by true optimization, when appropriate, yielded the most insightful and useful planning results. Pfizer most frequently utilized an iterative approach because, at any given time, one activity area (e.g., DC storage) was typically facing the most immediate operating challenges. Therefore, planners would explore options in this area in detail and then evaluate potential planned actions in this one area from a total network perspective to ensure that individual plans aligned with and improved overall network operations.

In closing, let's briefly return to the inventory planning component of this DSS. As noted, planners typically integrated the inventory decision support models with the other models shown in Figure 7.1 through the previously referenced iterative, scenario planning approach. Specifically, a series of strategic scenarios would be developed. These scenarios might propose alternative numbers of DCs for the network (e.g., three vs. two) and alternative locations, facility sizes, and material handling technologies. For each scenario, the inventory model would project the overall level of inventory investment requirements on the network. The projected network inventory investment would then be disaggregated to the DC level. These projections would facilitate both a calculation of the total inventory investment and carrying cost of each scenario and also serve as input to the DC storage model projections for individual scenarios.

This completes our brief review of selected key components of Pfizer's *strategic* and *tactical* Distribution Network DSS system. Over several years, this system provided key inputs to a number of long-run distribution studies and decisions including:

1. The determination of whether Pfizer should expand the first echelon of its two-echelon network into a larger echelon (e.g., expand from two regional DCs to three regional DCs)
2. The determination of a new pharmaceutical transport delivery mode network and
3. The determination of the best long-term US distribution network to serve Pfizer

Appendix

The following are several somewhat self-explanatory figures that illustrate the types of planning insights generated by the Pfizer strategic network planning DSS. Fictitious headlines for the figures are shown to illuminate how a logistics group would evaluate the outputs of a typical strategic network planning infrastructure analysis.

Briefly, Figures 7.4 to 7.6 illustrate the kind of results a DC network study would generate. These figures display sample outputs from a storage capacity scenario planning exercise evaluating requirements for the next five years, one of the major components of an overall network infrastructure study. These strategic planning exercises, conducted as a standard business process at least once a year, enabled Pfizer Logistics to plan for and meet future network requirements proactively. Briefly, for this particular scenario, these figures illustrate the following:

1. The current DCs lack the projected level of pallet storage capacity required over the next five years (Figure 7.4);
2. The projected storage capacity deficits vary significantly depending on what FGI inventory turns rate the firm is able to achieve (Figure 7.5); and
3. The potential costs of alternative network expansion configurations that would meet projected demand (Figure 7.6).

In actual practice, if a planning study produced projections such as those displayed in Figures 7.4 to 7.6 (i.e., a significant future network capacity deficit), this would trigger additional evaluations and the development of action plans, as appropriate.

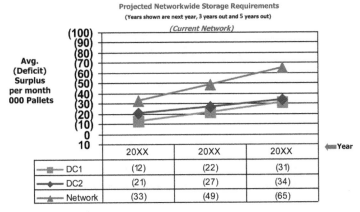

Figure 7.4 Simulation results reveal that the storage capacity of the current network will have to be increased significantly

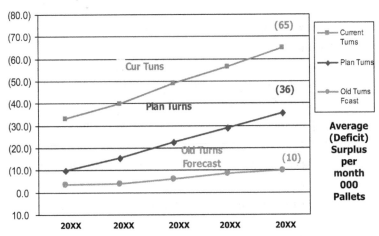

Figure 7.5 Current and future finished goods inventory turn rates significantly impact the magnitude of the required capacity expansion

- In the near-term, we can continue to use outside warehousing to supplement in-house capacity.
- A rough estimate of the facility expansion requirements and potential one-time costs are as follows:

Potential Expansion Requirements To Meet 20XX Requirements[1]				
Scenario	Pallet[2] Locations Added (000)		One-Time Expansion Costs $ (Millions)	Incremental One-Time Expansion Costs $ (Millions)
	Net Gain	Locations Added		
1. DC1, DC2 (Current)	65	65	$36	---
2. DC1, DC2, DC3	65	65	$62	$26
3. DC1, DC2**	65	110	$90	$54
4. DC1, DC2**, DC3	65	110	$110	$74

[1] Expansion requirements assume finished goods inventory turns remain constant through planning horizon
[2] Theoretical pallet locations increase. Operational factors may limit true "working gain" to 85%

- **Scenario 2 would add a new DC3.**
- **Scenarios (3) and (4) would both close the current DC2, and open a new DC2** location in (3), and a new DC2** and new DC3 in (4)**

Figure 7.6 Storage capacity requirements through 20XX will necessitate significant capital expansion projects

Monitoring Inventory Target and Excess Issues

A key operational responsibility of inventory planning and management consists of monitoring a firm's adherence to inventory targets and plans. There are numerous dimensions to this management component, including the following:

1. Developing appropriate FGI end item target levels by stocking location (i.e., at the SKU level);
2. Executing production and purchasing plans to maintain these targeted levels;
3. Monitoring customer service fill rates to ensure target rates are being met and that these targets are competitive; and
4. Monitoring and guiding overall firm FGI levels.

This list represents just a small sample of the many activities that comprise logistics inventory management in the short-run, operational planning horizon.

In this section, we will focus on one often overlooked management component of "monitoring and guiding" overall firm FGI levels: creating visibility across a firm when "excess inventory" becomes a prolonged problem. The authors have both observed and experienced situations at a number of firms where inventory levels far exceeded plans and major operational issues and extra-normal inventory expenses then ensued. There are usually many activities required to regain control of inventory levels without damaging customer service. One important step is to ensure that appropriate organizational awareness and concern exists at all management levels. Logistics managers must take responsibility for promoting this organizational visibility. In the remainder of this section, we present an analytic and reporting methodology that we have used successfully to generate widespread organizational awareness of serious excess inventory issues. We offer this in the hope that other practitioners facing similar environments may find this helpful.

Pictorial Description

The figures at the close of this section illustrate an analysis of a firm's FGI reviewed at the total firm, product family, and end item levels. The reader is encouraged to consider the headline of each figure as if he or she was reviewing a monthly report that had just been issued across the firm. The objective of this section is to suggest ideas to the reader on different analytic reporting formats to utilize in communications to his or her organization on the status of current inventory levels at his or her firm.

In reviewing these figures, assume that a logistics manager wishes to convey the magnitude and cost of the firm's current excess inventory positions.[16] Thus, the manager begins with several slides that communicate at an aggregate inventory/total pallet level the firm's current and recent historical positions (Figure 7.7). Then a comparison of actual inventory levels versus budget (Figure 7.8), and the total inventory housed in outside, third-party storage (Figure 7.9) follow. After this aggregate view, the logistics manager focuses on inventory at the product family and item level. Figures 7.10 and 7.11 detail the cost to the firm of its inventories and also highlight how many thousands of pallets of inventory above safety stock plus cycle stock targets there are by product. Finally, Figures 7.12 and 7.13 communicate the quantities of inventory on hand that are not generating any revenue, are literally inactive (e.g., are discontinued), or have been rejected for reasons such as product expiration. When presented effectively and regularly by logistics managers, reports such as these can rally an organization to take actions to bring its inventory down to appropriate levels.

---

[16]These reports are appropriate regardless of whether a firm's inventory level is low, high, or about right relative to targets. For illustration, we present a scenario where a firm's inventory levels are in excess.

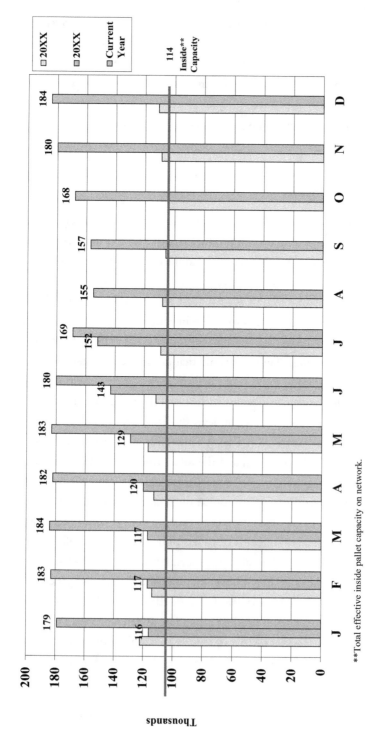

Figure 7.7 Historical total FGI—all locations average pallets in inventory per month

Thousands

Legend: ☐ 20XX   ☐ 20XX   ☐ Current Year

114 Inside** Capacity

J 179 116
F 183 117
M 184 117
A 182 120
M 183 129
J 180 143
J 169 152
A 155
S 157
O 168
N 180
D 184

**Total effective inside pallet capacity on network.

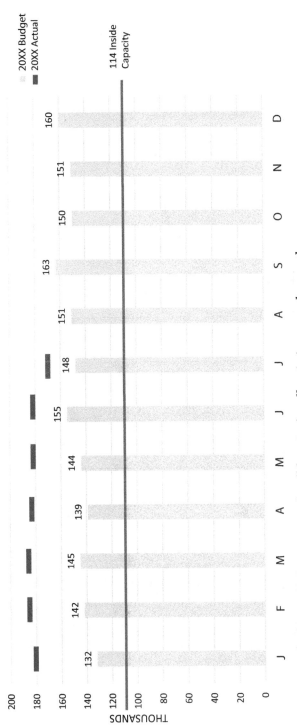

Figure 7.8 Total FGI: budget vs. actual—all location's pallets in inventory by month

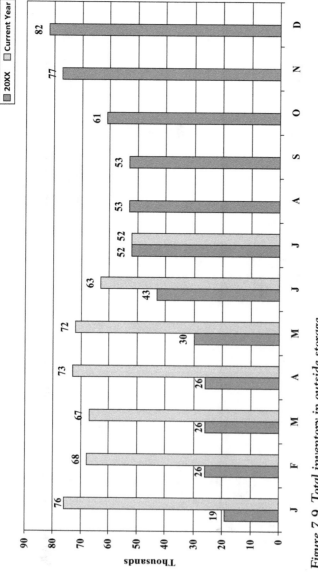

Figure 7.9 Total inventory in outside storage

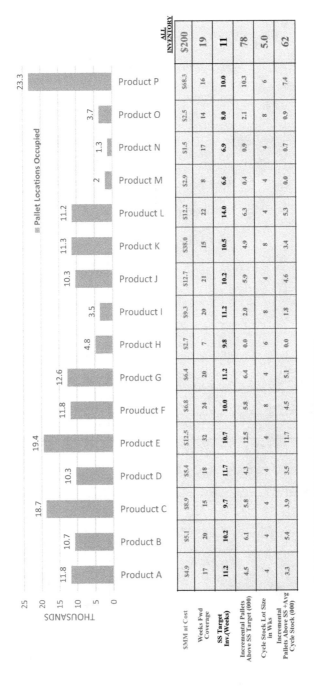

	Product A	Product B	Prouduct C	Product D	Product E	Prouduct F	Product G	Product H	Prouduct I	Product J	Product K	Prouduct L	Product M	Product N	Product O	Product P	ALL INVENTORY
$MM at Cost	$4.9	$5.1	$8.9	$5.4	$12.5	$6.8	$6.4	$2.7	$9.3	$12.7	$38.0	$12.2	$2.9	$1.5	$2.5	$68.3	$200
Weeks Fwd Coverage	17	20	15	18	32	24	20	7	20	21	15	22	8	17	14	16	19
SS Target Inv.(Weeks)	**11.2**	**10.2**	**9.7**	**11.7**	**10.7**	**10.0**	**11.2**	**9.8**	**11.2**	**10.2**	**10.5**	**14.0**	**6.6**	**6.9**	**8.0**	**10.0**	**11**
Incremental Pallets Above SS Target (000)	4.5	6.1	5.8	4.3	12.5	5.8	6.4	0.0	2.0	5.9	4.9	6.3	0.4	0.9	2.1	10.3	78
Cycle Stock Lot Size in Wks	4	4	4	4	4	8	4	6	8	4	8	4	4	4	8	6	5.0
Incremental Pallets Above SS +Avg Cycle Stock (000)	3.3	5.4	3.9	3.5	11.7	4.5	5.1	0.0	1.8	4.6	3.4	5.3	0.0	0.7	0.9	7.4	62

- The Weeks Forward Coverage given is the last forecast week for which this grouping has a forecast.
- SS Target Inventory = Safety Stock weeks forward coverage target

Figure 7.10 Total inventory and forward coverage

97

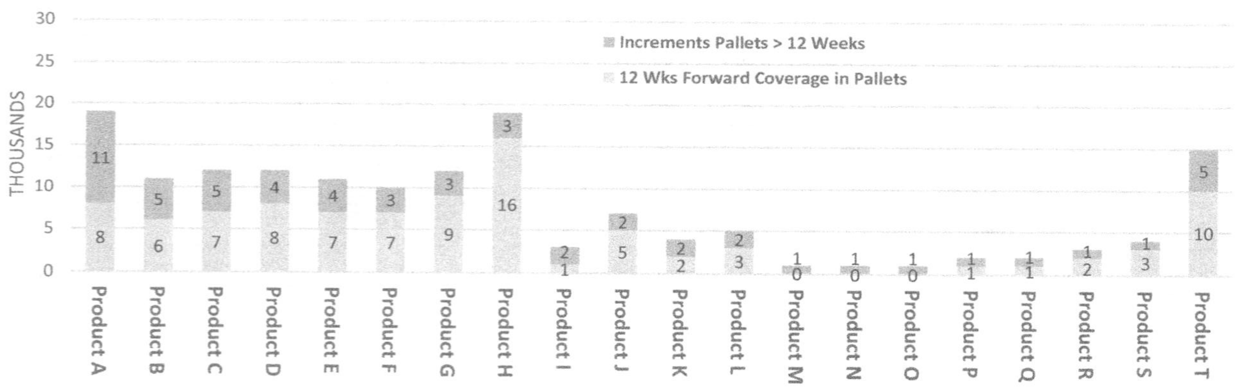

	Product A	Product B	Product C	Product D	Product E	Product F	Product G	Product H	Product I	Product J	Product K	Product L	Product M	Product N	Product O	Product P	Product Q	Product R	Product S	Product T
Cumulative Std Cost > 12 Wks (MM)	$7.6	$10.0	$12.6	$15.0	$19.5	$21.3	$22.6	$24.1	$27.7	$30.0	$34.3	$39.0	$41.4	$42.8	$46.5	$48.8	$50.3	$52.3	$52.7	$65.5
Cumulative Pallets > 12 Wks (000)	11.4	16.4	21.3	25.4	29.4	32.7	35.8	38.8	41.2	43.3	44.9	46.4	47.2	48.0	48.8	49.5	50.1	50.7	51.2	55.7

Based on inventory and forecast as of the beginning of the current month.

Figure 7.11 Products with 500 pallets or more of inventory in excess of 12 weeks' supply

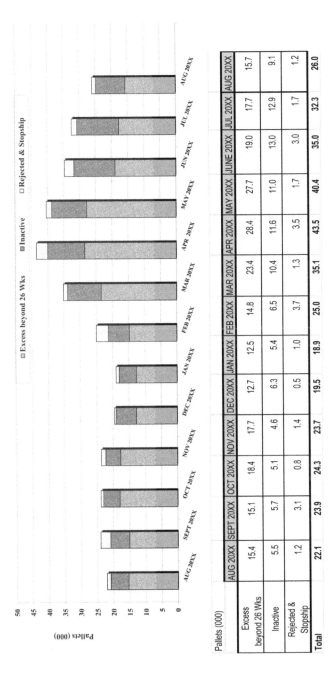

Pallets (000)	AUG 20XX	SEPT 20XX	OCT 20XX	NOV 20XX	DEC 20XX	JAN 20XX	FEB 20XX	MAR 20XX	APR 20XX	MAY 20XX	JUNE 20XX	JUL 20XX	AUG 20XX
Excess beyond 26 Wks	15.4	15.1	18.4	17.7	12.7	12.5	14.8	23.4	28.4	27.7	19.0	17.7	15.7
Inactive	5.5	5.7	5.1	4.6	6.3	5.4	6.5	10.4	11.6	11.0	13.0	12.9	9.1
Rejected & Stopship	1.2	3.1	0.8	1.4	0.5	1.0	3.7	1.3	3.5	1.7	3.0	1.7	1.2
Total	22.1	23.9	24.3	23.7	19.5	18.9	25.0	35.1	43.5	40.4	35.0	32.3	26.0

Based on inventory and forecast as of the beginning of the current month.

Figure 7.12 Non-Revenue generating inventory in pallets

Top 10 Excess Items

Items with more than 26 weeks of forward coverage.
Sorted by Pallets

Item No	Description	Item Type	Excess Pallets*
44335-01	Product 1	O/S	2,182
00504-00	Product 2	Club	875
00519-00	Product 3	O/S	600
00716-01	Product 4	Club	451
44305-00	Product 5	O/S	400
52122-00	Product 6	Promo	372
03339-00	Product 7	Club	369
65847-00	Product 8	Promo	364
60013-00	Product 9	O/S	362
22890-00	Product 10	O/S	357
Sum of Top 10 Excess:			**6,332**

*—Pallets beyond the first 26 weeks of forward coverage.

Top 10 Inactive Items

Items for which there is no forecasted demand.
Sorted by Pallets

Item No	Description	Item Type	Pallets	% Change vs Month Ago
65854-00	Product 1	Promo	474	0%
89919-01	Product 2	Promo	408	0%
44390-04	Product 3	Promo	330	-1%
42535-04	Product 4	Promo	274	0%
42163-00	Product 5	Promo	241	0%
48839-00	Product 6	Promo	213	0%
48837-00	Product 7	Promo	212	0%
70836-00	Product 8	Promo	211	-16%
00519-04	Product 9	O/S	205	0%
17215-00	Product 10	Promo	179	-46%
Sum of Top 10 Inactive:			**2,747**	

Based on inventory and forecast as of the beginning of the current month.

Figure 7.13 Top ten excess and inactive items

Summary

Inventory management is an extremely complex function that must be fully integrated with all other major components of logistics planning and management. In this chapter, we have presented methodologies to provide decision support and guidance to two major activities:

1. Integrated strategic and tactical logistics network and inventory planning, and
2. Monitoring and assuring visibility of inventory levels throughout a firm.

CHAPTER 8

Incorporating Feedback Loops into Logistics Decision Support

Introduction

In this chapter, we illustrate the concept of "feedback loops" in logistics processes. The role of feedback loops receives relatively scant attention; however, these tools represent an essential function in ensuring alignment between plans developed at different levels (e.g., the tactical and operational) and ensuring efficient operational execution.

We begin this chapter by describing what feedback loops are. We then offer an example of a manufacturing feedback loop, followed by an illustration of an inventory management feedback loop. We conclude the chapter with some brief summary comments.

What Is a Feedback Loop?

To define a feedback loop, let's briefly revisit the HMD framework discussed in Chapter 6 in the section titled "Strategic, Tactical, and Operational Manufacturing and Distribution Network Modeling". Figure 8.1 redisplays the HMD framework previously presented.

A distinguishing characteristic of a hierarchical planning framework is that decisions made at higher planning levels (e.g., the strategic level) place constraints and boundaries on subsequent decisions that will later be made at lower planning levels (e.g., the tactical level). This facilitates aligned decision making across all levels of a logistics organization and its individual functions from a "top-down" perspective. To strengthen the alignment of organizational decision making, "hierarchical" planning frameworks also employ "feedback loops." Briefly, feedback loops

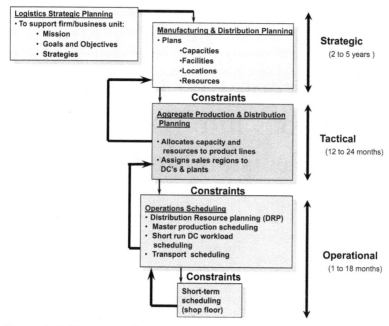

Figure 8.1 Hierarchical manufacturing and distribution planning framework

represent both formal and informal mechanisms by which planners at lower levels of the planning hierarchy provide feedback to planners at higher levels. In Figure 8.1, the arrows flowing from the operational level to the tactical level and from the tactical level to the strategic level represent feedback loops.

Feedback loops are one of the most important characteristics of a hierarchical logistics planning system. A true HMD framework is a closed loop system that employs a "top-down" planning approach complemented by "bottom-up" feedback loops. Given the emphasis of HMD systems on evaluating capacity levels and imposing and/or communicating capacity constraints from higher levels down to lower levels, it is imperative that strong feedback loops exist. As is well known, production and distribution plans that appear feasible at an aggregate level can often contain hidden infeasibilities that only manifest themselves at lower, more disaggregated levels. Without proper feedback loops embedded into a hierarchical planning framework, the danger that a logistics function will attempt to move forward with infeasible plans always exists. These infeasibilities often do not surface until an organization is in the midst of executing its operational plans and schedules.

Transferability and Importance of Feedback Loop Logic

From a "big picture" perspective, the ability to visualize and implement feedback loops represents an insightful and transferable skill set for a logistics manager. Why do we make this assertion?

Developing a good feedback loop requires a capability to understand how activities at a lower operating level work, interact with each other, and interact with and impact higher-level activities. This skill set is critical in all areas of business and management, whether it be logistics, marketing, finance, or other. Thus, the ability to envision the need for, and then to create, appropriate feedback and communication loops in a business operation is both critical and ubiquitous in its application.

Example 1: A Manufacturing Feedback Loop

Feedback loops from the operational level to the tactical level and from the tactical level to the strategic level represent a "key and defining attribute" of any hierarchical logistics planning system. To provide additional perspective of what a feedback loop is, we review an illustrative feedback loop from the family weekly production scheduling model to the PDCF model in Figure 6.3.[17]

In the tactical planning process, the PDCF model generates a 12- to 18-month production plan at the product family level for each plant in a network. The model also creates an integrated distribution plan that identifies which plants supply which DCs and which DCs serve which customers, again at the product family level. Figure 8.2 displays

---

[17]Some of the material presented in this section was originally published in Miller (2002) and is reprinted with the kind permission of Springer Science + Business Media.

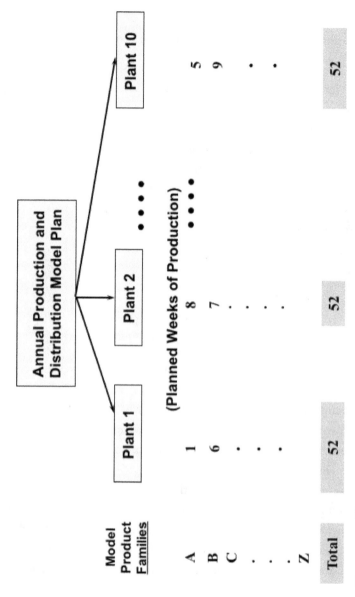

Figure 8.2 Illustrative tactical production plan created by the plant/DC/family optimization model

a network-wide annual production plan that for illustrative purposes, we will assume the PDCF model has created. This plan displays the weeks of production of each product family that each plant will manufacture over a 12-month planning horizon.

For illustration, we now focus on the PDCF model's assignment that plant 1 should produce 1 week of product family A. We will also assume that product family A has the following attributes:

1. It contains 20 finished good end items, and
2. Each of the 20 end items has a minimum production run length of a ½ day (i.e., if the plant has to produce an item, it must produce the item for a minimum of ½ of a day).

Briefly, end items are aggregated into product families for tactical planning on the basis of their respective similar characteristics. For example, assume that this is a ceramic tile manufacturing network such as the one discussed in Chapter 6 (i.e., AO's network), and that the 20 end items in product family A are 2" × 2" wall tile end items of different colors (blue, green, yellow, etc.). Each end item can be produced on the same production lines at the same plants and at very similar costs per unit and at similar output rates. These similar end items would be planned as one product family in the PDCF model at the tactical planning level.

Now let's consider Figure 8.3 which depicts two very different scenarios (Cases 1 and 2), under which the PDCF model could generate an initial assignment of 1 week of production for product family A at plant 1. The total demand for product family A consists of the sum of the demand for the 20 end items that comprise this product family. (For simplicity, we will also define production requirements as equal to total demand in this example.) Now consider Case 1 and Case 2 in Figure 8.3.

- *Case 1:* The total demand (and production requirements) for product family A at plant 1 is in three end items (1, 2, and 3).
  - There is no demand for end items 4 to 20 (i.e., demand = 0).

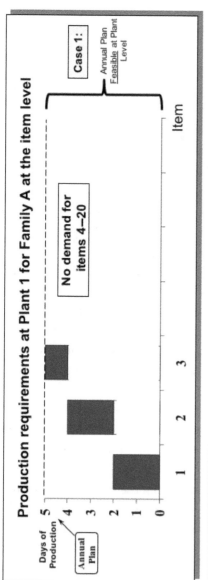
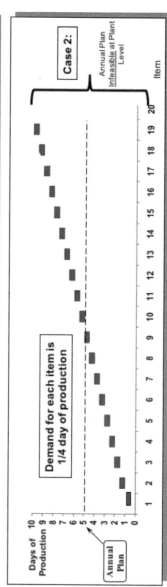

Figure 8.3 Two scenarios for product family A at plant 1

108

- Thus, as Figure 8.3 depicts, to satisfy the demand for product family A at plant 1 will require 2 days' production of item 1, 2 days of item 2, and 1 day of item 3.
- Therefore, plant 1 can feasibly produce the production assignment from the PDCF model of 1 week of family A. (Note that we define 5 business days as 1 week in this example.)

- *Case 2:* The total demand for product family A at plant 1 consists of ¼ of a day's production for each of its 20 end items.
  - $20 \times 1/4 = 5$ business days' total demand; or 1 week of demand (and production)—the assignment of the PDCF model to plant 1 for family A.
  - Recall, however, that plant 1 has a minimum production run length of a 1/2 day for any item.
  - Therefore, for plant 1 to produce all 20 items in family A will require $20 \times 1/2 = 10$ business days of production.
  - Thus, the production assignment from the PDCF model to plant 1 for product family A is not feasible.

How Infeasible Production Assignments Can Occur

At the network-wide tactical planning level, models and planners generally do not evaluate very detailed issues such as the minimum run length of individual end items at individual plants. The purpose and objectives of 12 to 18 months' planning exercises at the tactical level necessitate that planning/modeling be conducted at more aggregated levels (e.g., product families rather than end items). This allows the possibility that plans developed at the tactical level may in some cases be infeasible to implement at the operational level. Case 2 illustrates how these infeasibilities may arise.

In practice, "feedback loops" from lower planning and scheduling levels to higher levels take on great importance because of the type of situation illustrated in Case 2. As plans cascade down from one level to the next lower level (e.g., network-wide to individual plant), managers at the lower level must evaluate these plans and communicate back any infeasibilities. This becomes an iterative process whereby tactical plans should be revised based on feedback loop communications and then revised tactical plans reevaluated at the operational level. This process continues until a feasible plan, at all levels, is developed.[18]

Example 2: An Inventory Management Feedback Loop

Introduction

Feedback loops take many forms and can range from: (1) informal communications between two logistics functions, to (2) formal, standardized data input and output exchanges between functions, to (3) detailed mathematical algorithms that coordinate modeling assumptions and inputs between different planning and operating levels. This section will illustrate the need for a manufacturer to evaluate its inventory at the end item level across its entire network in order to determine the correct product family beginning inventory level inputs to its annual/tactical production planning process. Thus, the following is an example of a mathematical algorithm required to ensure synchronization between manufacturing and distribution inventory network operating conditions and annual/tactical production planning.

Manufacturing and distribution firms with thousands of unique finished goods end items typically develop their annual or tactical production and distribution plans at an aggregated product level. Numerous reasons exist for this planning approach, not the least of which is that it is often simply not practical or productive to develop long-run plans (e.g., 12 to 18 months) for thousands of individual end items. This is particularly the case for optimization-based annual production/distribution planning techniques, where by aggregating end items into product families, the planner can avoid creating models of unmanageable or mathematically intractable size.

---

[18]The reader is referred to Miller (2002) for additional discussion of feedback loops and hierarchical systems.

Product Line Structure

Figure 8.4 illustrates the levels of product aggregation that we assume. One can observe that end items tree up into product families and that product families then tree up into product lines. The example here assumes that the firm's annual production/distribution planning model defines products at the product family level (level 3 in Figure 8.4). As previously discussed, product families are created on the basis of the similarity of one or more key commonly shared characteristics of each end item within a family. In the production planning application for which the authors developed a detailed mathematical algorithm that incorporates the logic shown in this example, all end items within each family had virtually identical production rates, costs, and production possibilities.

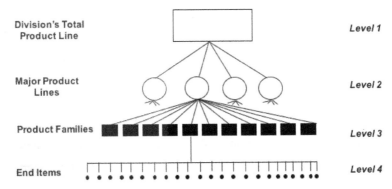

Figure 8.4 Product line structure

Why Is It Critical to Incorporate End Item Inventory Positions into Annual Product Family Level Production Plans?

It is necessary to evaluate current end item inventory positions over the entire manufacturing/distribution network in order to ensure that the firm's annual production plans do not underestimate total manufacturing capacity requirements. Inventory data, when developed at the product family level (rather than at the end item level), can provide misleading information leading to this underestimation of capacity requirements in long-run planning models.

To illustrate this, assume we are planning the annual production requirements of a product family that has five individual end items. Let us now consider the production requirements over a planning horizon for this product family when evaluated at two different levels of inventory aggregation: the end item level and the product family level. To measure the utility of a product family's current inventory, we require two definitions:

"Usable" inventory over the planning horizon is the minimum of:[19]

1. (forecast annual sales over the planning horizon) + (the end-of-period inventory target), or
2. The current (i.e., beginning-of-period) inventory.

"Excess" inventory over the planning horizon is the maximum of:[20]

1. (current or beginning-of-period inventory) − (usable inventory over the planning horizon) or
2. 0.

A comparison of Figures 8.5 and 8.6 reveals that the projected total production requirements over the planning horizon can vary substantially depending on whether one evaluates requirements at the end item level (Figure 8.5—11,000) or at the product family level (Figure 8.6—8,000). Further, the firm will underestimate its true production capacity requirements if it evaluates inventory at the product family level. In this example, the underestimate of capacity needs will occur because end item 5 has an extreme surplus of inventory that masks the current inventory deficits in items 1 to 4 of this family. Because item 5's current inventory exceeds the sum of its annual selling rate plus inventory target by 3,000 units, the firm will still have an inventory excess of 3,000 units in this item at the end of its 12-month planning horizon.

---

[19]In words, "usable" inventory is the amount of beginning inventory that can be used to meet forecast sales and the end of planning horizon ending inventory target.
[20]In words, "excess" inventory is the amount of beginning inventory (if any) that is not needed to meet the forecast sales and end of planning horizon inventory target.

	Total Production Requirements Over Planning Horizon (When Evaluated at End-Item Level)						
(1)	(2)	(3)	(4)	(5)	(6)	(7)
End Item	Beginning Inventory Position	Annual Selling Rate	End of Planning Horizon Inventory Target	Total Production Required Over Next 12 Months [a]	Useable Inventory Over Planning Horizon [b]	Excess Inventory Over Planning Horizon [c]
1	400	2,000	400	2,000	400	0
2	200	3,000	600	3,400	200	0
3	100	1,000	200	1,100	100	0
4	300	4,000	800	4,500	300	0
5	10,000	6,000	1,000	0	7,000	3,000
Total	11,000	16,000	3,000	11,000	8,000	3,000

a) calculation for column (5) = maximum of: [column (3) + column (4) - column (2), or 0].
b) calculation for column (6) = minimum of: [column (2), or column (3) + column (4)].
c) calculation for column (7) = maximum of: [column (2) - column (6), or 0].
  The planning horizon in this example is the next twelve months.
  Numbers in the "Total" row are the sum of the 5 individual item numbers in the column above them

Figure 8.5 Evaluating beginning inventory at item level

	Total Production Requirements Over Planning Horizon (When Evaluated at Product Family Level)				
(1)	(2)	(3)	(4)	(5)	(6)
Beginning Inventory Position	Annual Selling Rate	End of Planning Horizon Inventory Target	Total Production Required Over Next 12 Months [a]	Useable Inventory Over Planning Horizon [b]	Excess Inventory Over Planning Horizon [c]
11,000	16,000	3,000	8,000	11,000	0

a) calculation for column (4) = maximum of: [column (2) + column (3) - column (1), or 0].
b) calculation for column (5) = minimum of: [column (1), or column (2) + column (3)].
c) calculation for column (6) = maximum of: [column (1) - column (2), or 0].
* The planning horizon in this example is the next twelve months.

Figure 8.6 Evaluating beginning inventory at product family level

To plan production requirements accurately, the firm must recognize that it has 3,000 units of inventory in item 5 (and therefore in item 5's product family), which it cannot utilize over the planning horizon. For production planning purposes, including these 3,000 units in the product family's current inventory will overstate the true level of inventory "usable over the planning horizon" for this product family. Thus, the number displayed in column (6) of Figure 8.5 (8,000), rather than the number in column (5) of Figure 8.6 (11,000), represents the proper quantity to use as this family's "beginning-of-period inventory" in an annual production/distribution planning model. Obviously, for other reasons (e.g., financial, special marketing programs), one must account for this product family's excess inventory (over the planning horizon) in other planning areas.

The example in Figure 8.6 illustrates that evaluating inventory positions (and production requirements) at the product family level makes it impossible to recognize whether there is any excess or unusable inventory (over the planning horizon) in any of the end items within the product family. By using the approach shown in Figure 8.5, namely, evaluating inventory positions and production requirements at the end item level, and then summing the end item results to obtain product family requirements, one can accurately evaluate a product family's current level of "usable" inventory over the planning horizon.

Algorithm to Determine Usable and Excess Inventory over a Planning Horizon

The example in Figure 8.5 demonstrates the calculation of usable and excess inventory over the planning horizon for a stand-alone, one location manufacturing/distribution network. In the real world of multi-location networks, the determination of proper usable and excess inventory data for product families becomes more complex. However, the same basic logic used for the one location network can be extended to a multi-location, multi-echelon network.[21]

This section has presented a simplistic yet effective algorithm for developing beginning-of-period inventory data at the product family level for use in production/distribution planning models. Developing beginning-of-period product family inventory data using the approach described here creates the necessary link between long-run production/distribution planning and short-run, current inventory conditions.

---

[21]See Miller (1991).

Summary

In this chapter, we have illustrated two examples of feedback loops. Our first example linked network-wide tactical production planning and short-run manufacturing operations. We observed that a feedback loop between the two activities at different planning horizons facilitated a synchronized production plan across the network at the tactical and operational levels. Our second example again demonstrated that input from the operational level back up to the tactical planning level (i.e., a feedback loop) was required to identify the correct inventory data for long-run production planning.

CHAPTER 9

Using Activity-Based Costing in Logistics Decision Support

Introduction

Activity-based costing (ABC) has helped many companies for decades gain a true understanding of their costs to produce and distribute products to customers. ABC provides a precise, accurate view of costs at very granular levels, namely, at the individual product, service, and customer level. As we will discuss, this differs from traditional accounting systems that are best suited to generate cost analyses at the overall firm, function, and facility level but that distort costs at more granular levels such as the individual product or customer level.[22]

ABC receives relatively little attention in the world of logistics today, where such forces as the rapid advance of technology, the growth of e-commerce, and the rise of omni-channel dominate headlines and corporate resources. However, ABC remains a critical foundational tool that represents an absolute decision support necessity to ensure a firm can accurately understand its true costs to serve customers.

Background: What Is Activity-Based Costing

ABC first gained prominence in the corporate world during the 1980s as a new methodology that allowed manufacturers to accurately capture their true costs to produce individual products. Two of the original

---

[22]Some of the concepts and text in this section and the following section previously appeared in *Materials Handling and Logistics Magazine* (July 2017) and are presented here with the kind permission of MH&L.

developers of this approach, Robert Cooper and Robert Kaplan, described this methodology in a 1988 seminal article titled "Measure Costs Right: Make the Right Decisions."[23] These authors argued that because traditional accounting systems *proportionately* allocate a manufacturer's indirect overhead costs on the basis of gross measures such as the total dollar sales of each product produced, this results in distorted individual product cost calculations.[24] Further, when firms use aggregate measures to proportionately allocate costs such as marketing and distribution to individual products, the potential for major distortions in product costing increases dramatically.

Successes during the 1980s in applying ABC methods to manufacturing prompted an eventual expansion of this methodology to other key components of logistics (e.g., distribution). Firms such as Proctor & Gamble and WL began using ABC models to determine their overall costs of serving individual customers (e.g., Walmart) and of evaluating the costs of offering different individual services to customers (e.g., services such as vendor-managed inventory and advanced shipment notices—ASNs).[25] To illustrate how ABC decision support contributes to a firm's understanding of distribution and other related costs, let's consider the following example where a company is evaluating the profitability of its three major distribution channels.

A Distribution Channel Profitability Example

Assume company XYZ is a manufacturer and distributor of pharmaceutical and consumer products and that it sells its products through three primary distribution channels: mass merchandisers, wholesalers, and small retailers. Now let's evaluate the overall profitability of each channel on the basis of: (1) a traditional accounting system and (2) an ABC system. Assume that XYZ's traditional cost accounting system allocates its distribution center's (DC's) costs based on either the

---

[23]Cooper and Kaplan (1988)

[24]Indirect overhead costs are expenses such as heating, lighting, and supervisory management. In manufacturing operations, note also that direct labor costs, direct labor hours, and machine hours associated with producing individual products are other common "bases" or "drivers" for proportionately allocating overhead costs.

[25]See e.g., Liberatore and Miller (1998).

total dollars or weight shipped to each customer and channel. Typically, customers, channels, and products do not consume DC resources (such as labor and machine time) proportionately to their dollar or weight volume, so a traditional cost accounting system will distort the true costs. Suppose the XYZ DC distributes a mix of low-valued to high-valued products with a wide range in the dollar value per pound and that it receives, stores, and ships products in everything from individual eaches (e.g., pharmaceutical products) to pallet quantities (e.g., bulk consumer products). In addition, assume there are small pick lines (for eaches), automated conveyor lines (for cases), and forklifts (for bulk pallets) to move product from inventory storage to the shipping dock. Finally, there is a separate pick area to serve the special requirements of the three largest customers, and all modes of transport are used, from truckload to ground parcel to next-day air. An ABC view of costs at this facility would differ substantially from that of a traditional aggregate volume-based perspective.

Figure 9.1 shows the difference in the net profit generated by the three different distribution channels as calculated by traditional volume-based accounting and then by an ABC approach. In contrast to the "volume-driver" based accounting system that uses only sales dollars to allocate costs, XYZ's ABC system employs many more drivers. For example, the DC may use a case pick operation to serve small retailers and a bulk pick operation to serve wholesalers and mass merchandisers. The ABC system would accurately calibrate the different costs of serving customers using the two different operations. It would also evaluate the costs of all other major components such as order management, transportation, and sales force activities, involved in serving customers. In this fictitious case, one can observe that based on the ABC costing system, the small retailer channel provides the smallest profit margin (4 percent), while the mass merchandise (11 percent) and wholesale (9 percent) channels yield a higher return. Conversely, the traditional costing system incorrectly indicates that the small retailer channel generates the highest profit margin (16 percent), followed by the mass merchandise (9 percent) and wholesale (7 percent) channels, respectively. Note that in the traditional system, XYZ's $84-million total annual operating expenses are allocated to each channel on the

TRADITIONAL ACCOUNTING

	Mass Merchandisers $(MM)	Wholesalers $(MM)	Small Retailers $(MM)	Total $(MM)
Gross Revenue	400	200	100	700
Cost Of Goods	300	160	70	530
Gross Margin	100	40	30	170
Trade Promotions	16	2	2	20
Total Operating Expenses	48	24	12	84
Net Profit	36	14	16	66
Net Profit (%)	9.0%	7.0%	16.0%	9.4%

ABC COST-TO-SERVE

	Mass Merchandisers $(MM)	Wholesalers $(MM)	Small Retailers $(MM)	Total $(MM)
Gross Revenue	400	200	100	700
Cost Of Goods	300	160	70	530
Gross Margin	100	40	30	170
Trade Promotions	16	2	2	20
ABC Assignments:				
◆ Logistics Mgmt	8	4	5	17
◆ Order Mgmt	10	5	6	21
◆ Customer Mgmt	10	6	5	21
◆ Sales Force Activities	12	5	8	25
Total Operating Expenses	40	20	24	84
Net Profit	44	18	4	66
Net Profit (%)	11.0%	9.0%	4.0%	9.4%

Figure 9.1 Illustration of activity-based costing

basis of that channel's proportion of total gross revenue (e.g., the small retailer channel's operating expense equals 100/700 × $84 million). This gross allocation of operating expenses distorts XYZ's cost to serve each channel. This example illustrates the alternative, more accurate cost and profitability insights that an ABC system can generate and the dangers of making decisions using the volume-driver approach rather than an ABC system.

The ABC Models Underpinning ABC Systems

To develop an accurate ABC system, a firm must first develop a good process model of the activity or operation of interest. XYZ requires that its ABC system capture how its costs to deliver products to each customer differ. At the minimum, therefore, XYZ must create ABC models of its DC operations and transportation delivery processes. Further, as Figure 9.1 illustrates, XYZ is evaluating its costs by customer (and distribution channel) in terms of sales force activities and customer service. In practice, this would necessitate that XYZ construct and maintain process models of each of these major components of the order-to-delivery process. For illustrative purposes, we briefly consider DC operations, which represents one of the key activities of this overall process.

Figure 9.2 illustrates the process and cost model that XYZ would maintain for this operation. A team of DC operations and accounting/finance personnel would develop the process flows and cost analyses necessary to generate this model. A review of Figure 9.2 shows that the cost per unit (i.e., per pallet, case, or each) of every activity is calibrated. XYZ can combine this DC ABC model with its databases that provide data on how many cases, pallets, and eaches its DC picks and ships to each customer, in order to assess the costs XYZ incurs in serving each of its customers from the DC. XYZ would need similar models of the other major activities (e.g., transportation) utilized in serving its customers. Collectively, these ABC process models would facilitate XYZ's evaluation of the true cost of serving each customer.

Flow-Through Costing For A Distribution Center

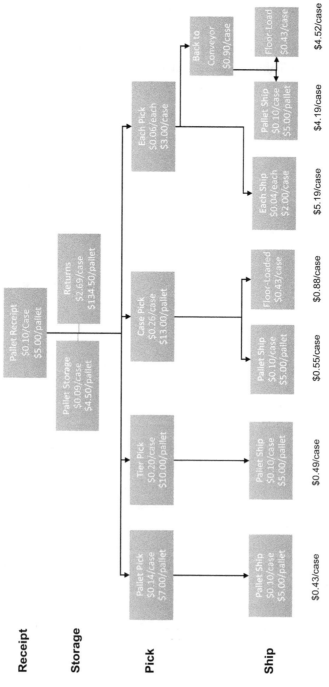

Figure 9.2 An ABC model of a DC operation

Source: Coyle, Langley, Novack and Gibson. Supply Chain Management: A Logistics Perspective, Cengage Learning, 10E

Why ABC Is More Critical Than Ever in Logistics Operations and Strategy

Omni-channel and the business-to-consumer (B2C) delivery process represents one of the most dynamic, rapidly evolving areas of logistics operations. Further, the escalating competition that B2C suppliers face in providing same or near-same day deliveries to consumers (often with no delivery fee) places many suppliers under severe cost pressures. Business to business (B2B) suppliers similarly face ever-increasing service demands and cost pressures, and many suppliers now compete in both the B2B and B2C worlds. To compete today, and to design efficient and profitable delivery strategies for tomorrow, requires suppliers to accurately know their costs of delivering *every product to every customer*. Suppliers managing without this essential information have little hope of designing and executing efficient and effective delivery network strategies and operations. Only suppliers armed with an accurate, ABC-based view of their delivery costs at the individual product and customer levels can successfully compete in the long run.

ABC Takeaways

There are several key takeaways we will briefly address in closing, and we offer additional references for the interested reader.

1. First, it is important to note that ABC costing systems are intended to *complement* traditional accounting and financial systems and should not be viewed as replacements or threats to a firm's existing systems. Rather, ABC systems facilitate detailed insights on a firm's true cost of serving individual products, offering specific customized services, and so on.

2. It is imperative that an ABC system utilize the same underlying data and database sources as the other accounting systems of a firm. ABC systems will employ the data differently and may have additional input sources than do the traditional accounting systems; however, the "total costs" of the two systems must be identical. In other words, any cost analysis generated by an ABC system must align with a firm's financial reporting system at an "aggregate level." As illustrated

in Figure 9.1, individual cost analyses (such as the cost of serving different distribution channels) will differ between the ABC and traditional accounting systems. However, at the aggregate operating cost level, the systems must agree.

3. To develop ABC models of its operations, a firm should utilize operational colleagues working with accounting/finance colleagues in a team-based approach. For example, to construct an ABC model of a DC, the project team should include several DC managers, as well as other logistics and accounting personnel.

4. Commercial software is available to facilitate the development and deployment of ABC systems, or, alternatively, a firm can develop its own ABC models to complement its existing accounting systems.

To conclude, in the rapidly evolving world of 21st century logistics, it is more critical than ever for firms to invest sufficient resources in the well-established, foundational decision support capability that an ABC DSS provides.[26]

Incorporating ABC into the Customer and Supplier P&L

The development of ABC models allows a manufacturer (supplier) to generate individual profit and loss (P&L) analyses of each of their customers. Conversely, the development of ABC models by a customer (e.g., a retailer) facilitates the creation of individual P&Ls for each of the customer's suppliers. Further, these individual P&Ls can then become key inputs to a supplier's initiative to establish a customer segmentation plan or a customer's plan to develop a supplier segmentation plan. In this section, we briefly outline this process.

Figure 9.3 displays an annual P&L generated by a manufacturer for a fictitious customer XYZ. A firm heavily committed to ABC will have individual models of some or all of the following logistics functions:

---

[26]Readers interested in learning more about ABC systems are referred to the references that follow as a good starting point: Chea (2011), Cooper and Kaplan (1988), and Liberatore and Miller (1998).

Customer XYZ Profitability Analysis – 12 Month P&L

Item	$	% To Sales	Item	$	% To Sales
1. Gross Sales	$66,942,069	102.6%	8. Direct Profit Contribution	$40,456,238	62.0%
2. Returns & Cash Discounts	$1,687,428	2.6%	9. Selling Expenses	$1,263,569	1.9%
3. Net Sales	$65,254,641	100.0%	10. Operations (including warehouse & order management)	$998,447	1.5%
4. Cost of Goods Sold	$16,208,665	24.8%	11. Operating Profit	$38,194,223	58.5%
5. Gross Margin	$49,045,976	75.2%	12. Write offs	$38,105	0.1%
6. Promotional Costs	$6,677,284	10.2%	13. Adjusted Operating Profit	$38,156,118	58.5%
7. Other Variable Expenses (including freight)	$1,912,454	2.9%			

Figure 9.3 An illustrative manufacturer's P&L for an individual customer

Source: Coyle, Langley, Novack and Gibson. *Supply Chain Management: A Logistics Perspective*, Cengage Learning, 10E

warehousing, transportation, order management/customer service, and manufacturing. Additionally, it might also have ABC models of non-logistics functions such as sales. All of these models can provide results at the individual customer and product level.[27] The annual costs of serving an individual customer or producing an individual product for a customer then become inputs to the customer's P&L.

A glance at Figure 9.3 shows the following:

1. The transportation costs of serving a customer, developed by an ABC model, would be input into line 7 (Other Variable Expenses),
2. The warehousing and order management/customer service costs, developed by other ABC models, would be input into line 10 (Operations), and
3. The costs of producing the products purchased by a customer, developed by another ABC model, enter line 4 (Cost of Goods Sold) of the P&L.

Additionally, the sales force-related cost of serving a customer, also developed by an ABC model, would appear on line 9 (Selling Expenses).[28]

A manufacturer that develops a P&L for each of its customers can use this data as input to construct a customer segmentation strategy. Figure 9.4 displays a typical customer segmentation scheme that manufacturers in industries such as consumer products frequently employ.[29] Customers in these four segments can be described as follows[30]:

1. *Protect:* those customers who are most profitable
2. *Build:* those customers who are relatively low cost to serve but whose annual purchases are relatively low

---

[27]ABC models are also frequently defined at other levels such as division, location, brand, and others (see e.g., Liberatore and Miller, 1998).

[28]To be clear, in addition to the logistics and sales activities, all the firm's other costs will also be found in this P&L.

[29]Figures 9.2, 9.3, and 9.4 are taken with permission from Coyle et al. (2017).

[30]Coyle et al. (2017), in their well-known logistics textbook, classify customers in these four segments using these descriptions.

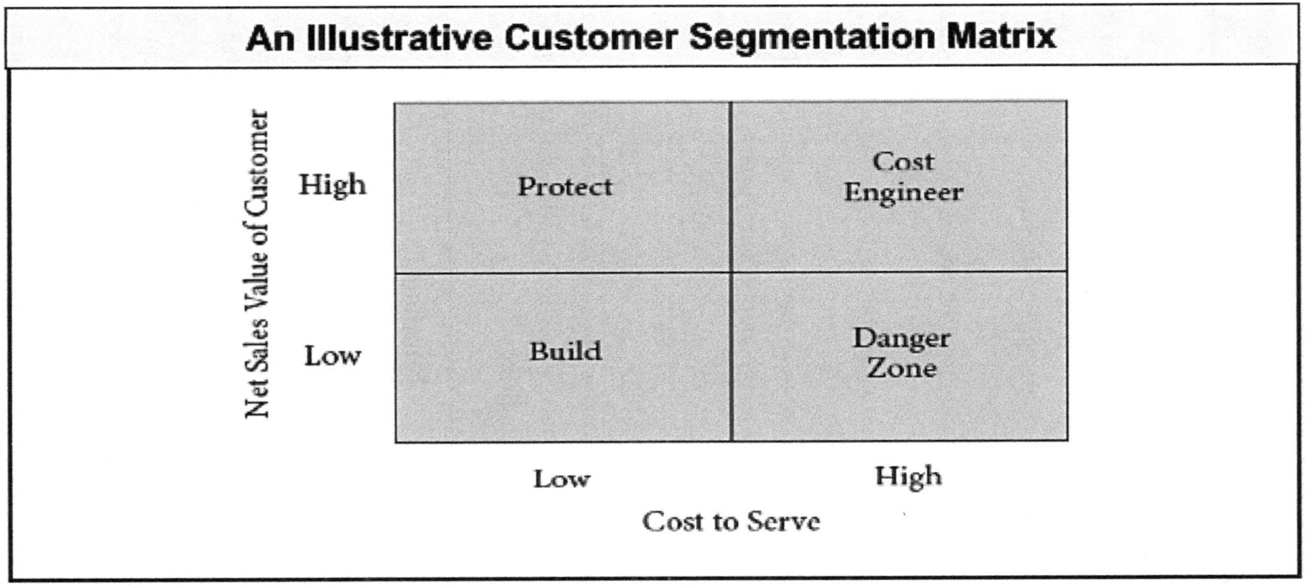

An Illustrative Customer Segmentation Matrix

	Low	High
High	Protect	Cost Engineer
Low	Build	Danger Zone

Net Sales Value of Customer

Cost to Serve

Figure 9.4 Illustration of a manufacturer's customer segmentation strategy

Source: Coyle, Langley, Novack and Gibson. *Supply Chain Management: A Logistics Perspective*, Cengage Learning, 10E

3. *Cost Engineer:* those customers whose annual purchases are high but who are also relatively costly to serve

4. *Danger Zone:* those customers who are the least profitable or may even be unprofitable to serve

The names ascribed to the first three segments convey, in general terms, the types of strategies a supplier would employ in working with customers in each segment. Briefly, for a customer in the fourth segment, "Danger Zone," a supplier's strategies might range from:

1. Developing a plan to improve the operational efficiency of the relationship, to

2. Charging the customer a higher price to cover the actual operational costs, to

3. Switching the customer to an alternative distribution channel (e.g., a wholesaler who carries the supplier's products).

Firms that employ customer segmentation strategies often also offer a menu of different services that customers can qualify to obtain on the basis of defined criteria such as annual sales levels or profitability. These firms then typically link their segmentation strategies and service menu options either directly or indirectly.[31]

Summary

One cannot overemphasize the fundamental role that ABC should play in a firm's logistics planning and strategy. ABC models provide a firm with penetrating insights on the true costs of customer service, production, and acquisition activities. Unlike high-level cost accounting systems, ABC models evaluate costs at the lowest, most granular activity level (e.g., picking a case in a warehouse). These models accurately differentiate costs

---

[31]A detailed discussion of customer segmentation and menu-based customer service strategies is beyond the scope of this book. However, the reader interested in further details on the development and use of these strategies is referred to Coyle et al. (2017) and Bowersox et al. (2013).

by customer, product, supplier, and many other dimensions, thereby facilitating better decision making, resource allocation, and strategy development. Finally, as noted, ABC models represent complementary decision support tools and must align with a firm's higher-level financial and cost accounting systems.

Part Two: Summary and Conclusion

Part Two has reviewed a broad range of logistics decision support methods, analytics tools, and frameworks. There exist numerous other DSS tools available to logisticians beyond these covered here. However, a logistics practitioner armed with the knowledge and understanding of the analytics and DSS capabilities presented in Part Two can easily adapt and incorporate other tools as needed. The wide swath of strategic, tactical, and operational DSS tools offered here illustrate how to incorporate any analytics methodology into an overall hierarchical planning framework and DSS.

PART III

Metrics and Techniques for Logistics Monitoring and Control

CHAPTER 10

Introduction

Objectives

In Part Three, we address two important questions of logistics management: How well are our logistics activities performing? What actions, if any, do we need to initiate to improve performance to better meet our goals? The first question relates to monitoring logistics performance, while the second addresses whether control is needed and, if so, what steps to take. Metrics are used to monitor and track performance, and then these can be compared with our goals. It is critical that a select set of metrics be chosen that best reflect our logistics operations and what we seek to accomplish. Here, we consider ways of organizing and selecting logistics metrics to best meet the needs of an organization.

Outline of Part Three

Following this brief introductory chapter, we next present in Chapter 11 a hierarchical framework for organizing logistics metrics and show how the framework can be applied to specific logistics functions, such as transportation and distribution. This framework addresses the need for metrics at the three hierarchical planning levels: strategic, tactical, and operational. We demonstrate at each level how the framework accommodates both metrics that are external, focusing on effectiveness, and internal, focusing on efficiency.

In Chapter 12, we illustrate how to create a customized index to monitor logistics operations. The advantage of creating a customized index is that a firm can track its overall logistics performance as one aggregated measure. We present a simple approach for developing the weights of the metrics that comprise the index. Additionally, the individual metrics comprising the index can be examined to determine the main drivers of changes in the index. In the Appendix, we present the Analytic Hierarchy Process (AHP) as an alternative method for developing the weights for the index. The advantage of the AHP is that it can facilitate the participation of senior managers in a structured group process to achieve consensus on the weights.

Finally, in Chapter 13 we present some techniques for monitoring operational transportation decisions. An example illustrates how diagnostic tools and reports can be used to monitor an organization's air-versus-ocean modal decision making on inbound replenishments to its distribution centers, leading to cost improvement opportunities. The approach presented is then extended to address monitoring outbound shipments to customers. We then close Part Three with a brief summary.

CHAPTER 11

Illustrative Logistics Performance Frameworks

Introduction

Selecting and monitoring key performance measurements is an important activity of logistics management. A well-designed performance management system facilitates: (1) monitoring how well the current logistics system is operating compared with targeted goals, and (2) if performance is not meeting the targets, then it provides the impetus to exercise control and, if necessary, implement adjustments to obtain alignment between actual performance and targeted goals.

As a result, the logistics organizations of many firms are increasingly employing an array of dashboards, scorecards, key performance indicators (KPIs), and/or other measurement indices to monitor their performance.[1] The development and availability of insightful measurements and metrics such as KPIs is a prerequisite for an effective performance management system. However, how a firm organizes its KPIs and how these KPIs align with its logistic management decision framework and strategy represents an equally important issue. Thus, not only must firms have strong KPIs, but these KPIs must align seamlessly with the firm's logistic management framework, activities, and strategy.

We present a hierarchical logistics performance (HLP) framework that can enable a firm to synchronize its logistics management plans and decisions with performance measures that monitor the impact of actions taken. This framework provides a vehicle to house a firm's

---

[1]Firms are increasingly employing the term "control tower" to describe this array of performance monitoring tools.

strategic, tactical, and operational logistics performance measures. These measures, or typically KPIs, can be monitored using a scorecard or dashboard, as shown in Table 11.1 and Figure 11.1, respectively. We illustrate how this hierarchical performance framework aligns with a firm's logistics management activities at all three planning levels. We then show how the framework can be applied to specific logistics functions.

Table 11.1 *Example of a logistics scorecard*

KPI	2018 (%)	2019 Goal (%)	2019 Month actual (%)	2019 YTD actual (%)
On-time delivery	86.7	88.0	89.9 ▲	79.2 ▼
Retail in stock	97.4	97.5	96.9 ▼	97.2 ▲
Distribution-to-store fill rate	95.1	95.5	94.5 ▼	94.2 ●
Case fill rate	96.2	97.6	94.4 ▼	95.3 ▼
Display case fill rate	98.0	98.0	98.3 ▲	97.3 ▼
Over, short and damaged	0.29	0.35	0.21 ▼	0.21 ▲
• Triangle facing up means better than last month or last year to date, triangle facing down means worse than last month or last year to date, circle means the same as last month or last year to date				

A Hierarchical Logistics Performance Framework[2]

We begin by distinguishing between measures, metrics, and indices as used in performance management and how they relate to KPIs. A *measure* requires no calculations and has simple dimensions. Some logistics examples include units of inventory and back-order dollars. A *metric* requires a calculation or a combination of measures, often in the form of a ratio. Logistics examples include inventory future days of supply, inventory turns, and sales dollars per stock keeping unit (SKU). An *index* combines two or more metrics into a single indicator, usually used to track trends in the outputs of a process. Two logistics examples are a perfect order fulfillment

---

[2]Portions of sections "A Hierarchical Logistics Performance Framework" and "Applying the Hierarchical Performance Framework to Specific Logistics Functions" draw upon concepts originally introduced in Liberatore and Miller (2012).

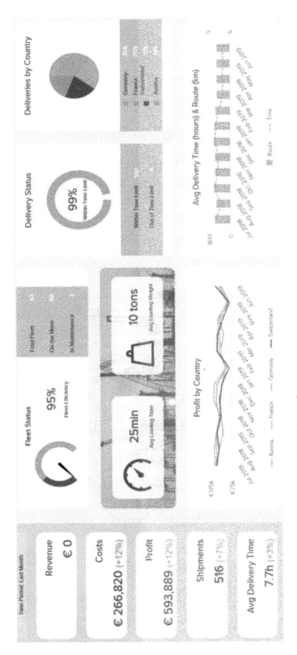

Figure 11.1 Example of a logistics dashboard

Source: Screenshot from Datapine (2019), www.datapine.com/dashboard-examples-and-templates/logistics

index and a facility utilization index for a network of plants. A performance management system is typically comprised of a set of measures, metrics, and indices. Since metrics and indices utilize measures, we will use the term *measure* when a measure, metric, or index might be appropriate. A KPI is a metric that your organization has identified as one that is closely aligned with your objectives, one that closely tracks or predicts performance. Some often-used logistic performance metrics and indices are listed in Table 11.2.

Table 11.2 *Frequently used logistics metrics*

Metric	Description
Perfect order fulfillment	Percentage of orders that are error free
Customer order cycle time	Average difference between actual delivery date and customer purchase order creation date
Order Fill rate	Percentage of a customer's orders that are filled in full on the first shipment
Freight bill accuracy	Percentage of freight bills that are error free
Freight cost per unit	Freight cost per item or SKU
Average payment period for production materials	(Materials payable divided by total cost of materials times) × days in the period
Cash-to-cash cycle time	Average difference between materials order payment date and customer payment date
Gross margin ROI	(Gross profit divided by average inventory investment) × 100
Days sales outstanding	(Receivables divided by sales) × days in the period
Turn-earn index	(Inventory turnover ratio divided by gross margin percentage) × 100
On-time shipping rate	The percentage of times that shipments arrive on or before the requested ship date
Inventory turnover ratio	Cost of goods sold divided by average inventory investment
Inventory days of supply	Inventory on hand divided by average daily usage
Days of supply	(Average inventory divided by monthly demand) × 30
Inventory velocity	Opening stock divided by next month's sales forecast

Logistics performance management is needed for monitoring and control at three levels: strategic, tactical, and operational. In previous discussions of logistics planning in this book (Chapter 1), these three levels were differentiated by their time horizon: long run, intermediate, and short run, respectively. In our HLP framework, the scale or relative magnitude of an operation or activity that a performance measure monitors determines where it fits in the hierarchy. Within each of the three levels of the HLP framework, we further differentiate performance measures as either external or internal. *External measures* focus on the effectiveness of a firm's shipments or flows across its network and to customers, while *internal measures* evaluate a firm's efficiency in producing or delivering its outputs and services. Typical external performance metrics are order and line item fill rates on customer orders. For example, when a mass merchandiser places an order to a product supplier, these metrics track whether the supplier delivers the total order and the individual items, respectively, on time and complete as ordered. However, these external metrics do not evaluate the supplier's order delivery cost, such as whether the order was delivered on time but by expensive air freight rather than originally planned surface transportation because of a production delay. In this instance, while the order delivery was effective (i.e., it met the customer's time requirement), it was not efficient (i.e., it was more costly than a normal surface delivery). Internal performance metrics such as "distribution cost per case" and "freight cost per pound" would be adversely affected by using the more expensive air delivery mode, if surface delivery is the normal mode planned for a lane.

Figure 11.2 displays the HLP framework, showing the three levels (strategic, tactical, operational), and the two measurement perspectives (external and internal). At the strategic level from an external perspective, this framework spans the firm's facilities network, through plants, distribution centers, customers, and consumers. From the internal perspective at the strategic level, we include the firm's top-level functions related to logistics, such as distribution. At the tactical level, performance measures are required for such activities as warehouse operations and transportation, since these are the key functions of distribution. Drilling down into warehouse operations, we see from Figure 11.2 that it has five major subfunctions or processes at the operational level: receiving, putaway, storage,

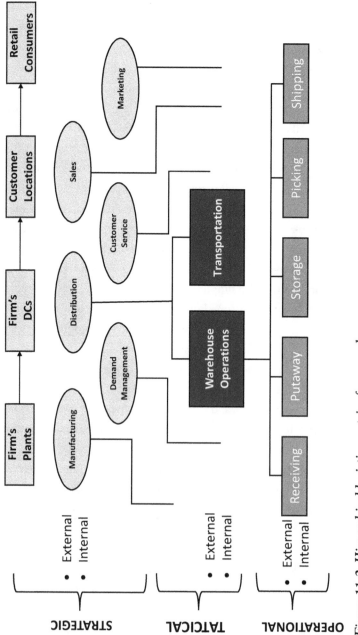

Figure 11.2 Hierarchical logistics metrics framework

picking, and shipping. Internal and external performance measures are required at each level in this framework.

Applying the Hierarchical Performance Framework to Specific Logistics Functions

Figure 11.3 indicates how internal and external performance measures are set across the three levels of the HLP framework, continuing with distribution as our example. For the distribution organization (strategic level), percentage of scheduled customer shipments delivered on time, and the average and variance of order cycle lead time represent external metrics, since they help to measure flows across the supply chain. They are strategic since they address the mission of the distribution function, ensuring delivery of products and services to customers in a timely manner. The total distribution cost per unit delivered is an internal, strategic metric since it measures the efficiency of distribution at the highest organization level.

At the tactical level, the percentage of lines or orders picked correctly, and the percentage of orders picked on the scheduled day, represent external metrics because they evaluate the impact of warehouse operations across the supply chain. When a warehouse picks an order correctly, it contributes to the ultimate successful delivery of products to a customer who has placed an order. Similarly, when a warehouse picks an order on the scheduled day, this contributes toward a successful on-time delivery of products to a customer. The third tactical metric shown in Figure 11.3, total warehouse costs per unit of throughput, represents an internal metric, since it offers a summary view of the internal cost (and efficiency) of the warehouse operation.

Focusing on the warehouse receiving function at the operational level, the percentage of cases (or lines) received correctly (i.e., accurately) is an example of an external performance metric. We categorize this metric as external because the accuracy with which this function receives inbound shipments will impact the next stage of the logistics flow. For example, suppose that the receiving area miscodes an inbound receipt as product A, when in fact it received a delivery of product B. If this error remains undetected, this inventory of product B will then be put away into inventory

Measure:

Level:	Type:	

Distribution

Strategic — External
- Percentage of scheduled customer shipments delivered on-time
- Order cycle lead time: from release to distribution to customer delivery
  - ➤ time in days   - variability

Strategic — Internal
- Total distribution cost per unit delivered

Warehouse Operations

Tactical — External
- Percentage of lines/orders picked correctly
- Percentage of orders picked on scheduled day

Tactical — Internal
- Total warehouse costs per unit of throughput

Receiving

Operational — External
- Percentage of cases/lines received correctly

Operational — Internal
- Total receiving costs per unit

Figure 11.3 Illustrative hierarchical performance measures for distribution function

classified as product A. Then, at some future point, this product could be picked and delivered to a customer who ordered product A, thereby creating a customer service issue, since the product delivered would really be product B (and not A as ordered). Therefore, the percentage of lines or cases received correctly is classified as an external measure. In contrast, total receiving cost per unit has an internal orientation and will be of most immediate concern to receiving and warehouse personnel.

As another brief example, consider manufacturing, which is slotted at the strategic level in Figure 11.2. A major manufacturing function such as fabrication would be at the tactical level, with fabrication subfunctions such as machining placed at the operational level (not shown in Figure 11.2). Manufacturing cost per unit would be an example of an internal performance metric at the strategic level, processing cost per unit would be an internal metric at the tactical level, while item defect rate would be an external metric at the operational level.

The HLP framework offers several important benefits. First, it provides a unified framework for aggregating performance measures across an organization. It enables a firm to organize its key performance measurements into a structure that leads to a relatively few, high-level, strategic measures (e.g., between 10 and 25) that monitor overall firm performance. These are sometimes referred to as KPIs. Second, this structure facilitates having additional performance measures that monitor smaller components of a firm's operation that align with overall firm objectives. In this way, all functional areas can develop and maintain their own measures and contribute to an overall measurement system. In addition, each function can then focus on a few key measures to help improve its performance. Finally, the HLP can contribute toward aligning the collective activities of a firm to meet a desired mission and set of objectives. For example, if a firm has a comprehensive measurement system in place that covers its major functional areas, managers can view the system in its entirety to identify any potential misaligned activities or objectives.

Summary and Conclusion

In this chapter, we discussed the need for organizations to use KPIs and other measurements to help monitor and control logistics operations.

We presented examples of scorecards, dashboards, and commonly used metrics. A HLP framework for organizing logistics measures was developed and addressed the strategic, tactical, and operational levels. This framework accommodates external metrics, such as order and line fill rate, which focus on effectiveness, as well as internal metrics, such as distribution cost per case and freight cost per pound, which focus on efficiency. This framework and its use of internal and external measures can be applied to specific logistics functions, with transportation and warehouse operations provided as examples. Advantages of the framework include the ability to: (1) aggregate measures across the entire organization; (2) focus on a few key strategic measures; and (3) establish a set of measures targeted for specific logistics functions, in a way that all measures are aligned with the achievement of the company's mission and objectives.

CHAPTER 12

Creating Customized Indices to Monitor Logistics Operations

Introduction

A logistics performance index (LPI) can be used to monitor the firm's progress in managing its logistics activities. It can also be linked to an organization's planning process to determine how well it is achieving its strategies and objectives. The KPIs that are most closely linked to the organization's strategy and objectives or management priorities should be included in the index. An advantage of creating an LPI is that overall logistics performance is represented by a single aggregate measure that offers managers an initial, high-level logistics perspective.

The LPI is a weighted average of the points associated with all the KPIs that comprise the index. The individual weights provide the relative importance of each KPI in contributing to the LPI. These weights can be developed through discussions with the logistics planning and/or management team or during the strategic planning process. One approach for developing the weights is to allocate 100 points across the KPIs and is the approach shown here. An alternative approach that offers several advantages is to apply the AHP, which is discussed in the Appendix of this chapter. For our example, we will use a representative set of KPIs, drawing from those discussed in Chapter 11 to create an LPI. An explanation of the process of determining the LPI follows.

Constructing the Index

The first step is constructing a baseline value or score for the index in an initial or baseline period such as the first quarter of 2019. The baseline value provides an index score against which we can then measure the value of the index in subsequent time periods. Table 12.1 illustrates the computation of the baseline index. The value for the Baseline Quarter represents the actual value of the KPI during the initial time period. For example, 93 percent is the baseline value for perfect order fulfillment. To initiate the baseline index, each KPI is assigned 100 points. That is, a 93 percent value of perfect order fulfillment is linked to 100 points. To determine the baseline value of the LPI we multiply each KPI's baseline points (100 in all cases) by its weight and then sum the results. Note that, by construction, the baseline value of the LPI is always 100, since the weights sum to 100 percent.

We can now compute the LPI for the next quarter. For each KPI, we must determine its percentage change (positive or negative) over the baseline and then multiply the result by the baseline points to determine the adjustment points required. The adjustment points are combined with the baseline points to determine the next quarter's points. The calculation is much simpler than it sounds. For example, from Table 12.1 we see that perfect order fulfillment favorably increased from 93 to 94 percent. We determine its change over the baseline by using the formula: 100 × (New KPI value − Baseline KPI value)/Baseline KPI value, or 100 × (94 − 93 percent)/93 percent, or a 1.08 percentage improvement. Therefore, the perfect order fulfillment points for next quarter are 100 + 1.08 percent × 100, or 101.08. The same process can be used for all KPIs, where an increase in value represents an improvement in performance, specifically, the nonitalicized KPIs in Table 12.1. However, for the remaining (italicized) KPIs in Table 12.1, our calculation process must change because a *decrease* in value is an improvement in performance. For example, customer order cycle time improved from the baseline to the next quarter since it *dropped* from 5 to 4 days. We determine its change over the baseline by *reversing* the order of the two terms in the numerator of our formula: 100 × (Baseline KPI value − New KPI value)/Baseline KPI value. Therefore, customer order cycle time improved by 100 × (5 − 4)/5, or 20 percent over the baseline, and so the points for the next quarter are 100 + 20 percent × 100 = 120.

Once all the KPI points for the next quarter are determined, we can compute the LPI for the next quarter by multiplying each KPI's points in

Table 12.1 *Example of a logistics performance index*

KPI definition	Baseline quarter			Next quarter		
	Value	Points	Weights	Value	Points	Weights
Perfect order fulfill-ment (%)	93%	100	0.15	94%	101.08	0.15
Customer order cycle time (days)	5	100	0.10	4	120.00	0.10
Customer order fill rate (%)	95%	100	0.10	93%	97.89	0.10
Cash-to-cash cycle time (days)	30	100	0.12	31	96.67	0.12
Distribution-to-store fill rate (%)	90%	100	0.10	88%	97.78	0.10
Inventory turnover (value)	8	100	0.11	7.5	93.75	0.11
Inventory carrying cost/inventory value (%)	20%	100	0.07	19%	105.00	0.07
Case fill rate (%)	96%	100	0.10	95%	98.96	0.10
Logistics manage-ment cost/$100k revenue (%)	9%	100	0.08	8.50%	111.11	0.08
Over, short & dam-aged (%)	0.30%	100	0.07	0.28%	106.67	0.07
	Baseline Index = 100.00			Next Quarter's Index = 102.24		

Note: If a KPI definition is italicized, improved performance is indicated by a decrease in the KPI Value

the next quarter by the same weights used to compute the baseline index and then summing the results. In our example as shown in Table 12.1, the overall change in performance was good, increasing from the base-line index value of 100 to next quarter's index value of 102.24. This 2.24 percent increase indicates that the firm has made significant progress in executing its logistics activities. The individual KPIs comprising the LPI can be examined to determine the main drivers of the changes (if any) in its value. For example, the improvement to customer order cycle time led to an increase in the LPI of $(120 - 100) \times 0.10 = 2.00$ points, while the reduction in inventory turnover led to a $(100 - 93.75) \times 0.11 = 0.69$ drop in the index. Over time, the change and rate of change in such an index provides a quantitative perspective on overall progress. The LPI can be included in a dashboard used to track logistics activities.

Summary

In this chapter, we have shown how to create a customized index to monitor the firm's progress in achieving its logistics objectives. An advantage is that overall logistics performance can be monitored by a single aggregate measure that provides a high-level perspective. KPIs would also be used to monitor logistics activities at the strategic, tactical, and operational planning levels.

Appendix: Applying the Analytic Hierarchy Process to Develop a Customized Logistics Index

The AHP can be applied to develop the KPI weights for a customized logistics index. The AHP enables all members of the logistics management team to participate in a group process to develop a consensus set of weights. As an example, the KPIs from Table 12.1 can be organized to support two logistics objectives: efficiency and delivery effectiveness, as shown in Figure 12.1. These objectives, in turn, support the overall logistics management goal. To determine the KPI weights, the AHP requires the management team to make a set of relative judgments, called *pairwise comparisons,* at each level of the AHP framework, namely, the importance of the objectives in achieving the goal and the importance of the KPIs in achieving each objective. The results are then combined using a weighted averaging approach to determine the KPI weights.

For example, in applying the AHP process, one question might be as follows: with respect to achieving the logistics management goal, which objective, efficiency, or delivery effectiveness is more important— and how much more important is it? Each member of the management team would then answer this question using the AHP's 1–9 numerical scale. Briefly, in this scale, a value of 1 means that the two objectives are equally important in achieving the logistics management goal. A value of 3 for efficiency relative to delivery effectiveness (i.e., 3:1) would indicate that efficiency is a moderately more important objective than delivery effectiveness in achieving the goal. Choosing the values 5, 7, or 9 would mean that efficiency is strongly, very strongly, or extremely more important, respectively, as compared with delivery effectiveness. Intermediate values can be used, so, for example, a value of 2 would mean equally to moderately more important. Thus, in the AHP scale, the higher the value assigned to any relative judgment or pairwise comparison, the more important the first item is relative to the second item.

The individual judgments of the management team members are mathematically combined to obtain the consensus judgment used in the analysis.[3] In this case, since there are only two objectives, one relative judgment is needed. Assume that the consensus judgment of the management team is 1.5, indicating that efficiency has a score of 0.60 and delivery effectiveness has a score of 0.40 (0.60/0.40 = 1.5).

Next, each team member would make a series of comparisons or relative judgments addressing the extent to which the KPIs achieve the efficiency objective. For example, one question might be: with respect to the efficiency objective, which KPI, cash-to-cash cycle time or inventory turnover, is more—and how much more important is it? Since there are five KPIs supporting the efficiency objective, ten relative judgments would be needed to cover all KPI pairs, although the AHP will still work if a specified smaller set is provided.

Once all the judgments relating to the efficiency KPIs are collected, a mathematical formula is applied to assign relative scores for each of the KPIs. The combined scores will sum to one, allowing for easy comparison. For example, cash-to-cash cycle time might have a score of 0.20; inventory turnover, 0.15; and so on. To obtain a KPI's overall weight, its efficiency score is multiplied by the score of its objective in achieving the goal. For example, since efficiency's score is 0.60, cash-to-cash cycle time will have a final weight of 0.60 × 0.20 = 0.12, which

---

[3]The geometric mean is generally used to combine AHP judgments. For example, suppose there were five judgments that needed to be combined: 2, 1, 2, 1, and 2. The geometric mean is $(2 \times 1 \times 2 \times 1 \times 2)^{1/5}$, which equals 1.5. These calculations are performed within AHP software packages such as Expert Choice (www.expertchoice.com) and Super Decisions (www.superdecisions.com).

will be used in the customized index. The same approach would be used to determine the overall weight of KPIs that support the delivery effectiveness objective.

AHP software packages such as Expert Choice (www.expertchoice.com/ ahp-software) or Super Decisions (https://superdecisions.com/) can simplify the elicitation of the comparisons and automatically perform such calculations. However, regardless of whether a formal prioritization process such as the AHP is used, an important task of the logistics management team is to select and track logistics KPIs for monitoring and control, and it is helpful to combine them into a customized index to track overall performance.[4]

Figure 12.1 Example of an AHP metrics hierarchy

---

[4]Readers interested in learning more about the AHP are referred to Saaty (1996) for a complete exposition of the method. Miller and Liberatore (2011) discuss how the AHP can support the supply chain strategic planning process, while Liberatore and Miller (1998) show how the AHP can link the balanced scorecard and activity-based costing to logistics strategy. Liberatore et al. (1992) use the AHP to link capital budgeting to business strategy, and Liberatore (1987) shows how the AHP can be applied for project selection.

CHAPTER 13

Techniques for Monitoring Day-to-Day Transportation Decisions

The Manufacturing and Distribution Network

In this chapter, we consider several approaches for monitoring and controlling transportation activities. We begin with an air-versus-ocean operational monitoring system. To facilitate this and a second example that will follow it, we consider a hypothetical firm (Firm XYZ) operating the manufacturing and distribution network depicted in Figure 13.1.

Firm XYZ operates several plants that supply three regional distribution centers (DCs) located in the United States. Each of the firm's plants is located offshore. Firm XYZ's regional DCs distribute finished goods to customers in the United States via local depots/transshipment points. (We will consider the outbound to customer deliveries from these depots in more detail shortly.)

The firm has previously analyzed its network and determined that its plants should ship products to its three U.S. regional DCs utilizing ocean container transport. Thus, the firm's normal replenishment mode consists of three linked "surface" moves: (1) plant to port (via truck), (2) port to port (via ocean container) and (3) port to DC (via truck).

As is frequently the case under such a scenario, Firm XYZ will use air freight rather than ocean transport to replenish its regional DCs in situations where conditions dictate that an exception be made to the normal replenishment mode. For example, when a DC runs low on inventory of key items, planners may utilize faster air freight to replenish inventories as soon as possible.

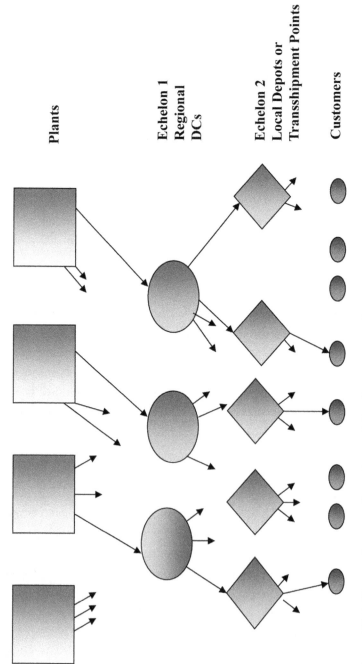

Plants

**Echelon 1
Regional
DCs**

**Echelon 2
Local Depots or
Transshipment Points**

Customers

Figure 13.1 *Illustrative manufacturing and distribution network*

In practice, one finds in numerous industries that firms employ expensive air freight in many one-off cases where less expensive but slower ocean freight would suffice.[5] Therefore, in situations where a firm's policies allow the substitution of air transport for ocean freight, firms often find it advisable to monitor their daily ocean-versus-air decision making.

Monitoring Inbound Transportation Decisions: Use of Air Freight

Table 13.1 displays an illustrative chart that a firm's planners can maintain, at an aggregate level, to monitor daily transport mode decisions. For all shipments made year to date and for the most recent month, it summarizes the "weeks' forward coverage" inventory of an item that was available in a DC at the time an air shipment occurred, providing insight as to whether the firm is utilizing air freight effectively. To better understand the purpose of this table, assume that it takes 2 weeks by ocean to transport finished goods to Firm XYZ's U.S. DCs from its offshore plants. Also assume that it takes only 2 days by air to ship products from the plants to the DCs. Recall that ocean is the "normal" or "standard" replenishment mode.

On a regular basis (e.g., monthly) managers should review Table 13.1 for each DC. If this summary table shows that most or all air freight is occurring in cases where inventory at a DC is quite low (e.g., perhaps 4 weeks or less), this generally indicates that air freight is being used appropriately. However, if Table 13.1 shows that air shipments are frequently occurring when a DC already has many weeks' forward coverage available in-house (e.g., greater than 8 weeks), this likely indicates an overuse of expensive air transport and, as we will illustrate shortly in Table 13.2, should alert managers to investigate further.

The illustrative data in Table 13.1 shows that for the year to date over 50 percent of air freight shipments to XYZ's DC #1 have occurred when this DC already had 8 weeks or more forward coverage in-house of the items shipped by air. Given that normal ocean transport replenishes the DCs from the plants in just 2 weeks, this report alerts the firm that it is unnecessarily utilizing expensive air freight. In practice, the next step

[5]See Gupta et al. (2002).

Table 13.1 *Summary of air freight costs and inventory availability when air shipments occurred*

Firm XYZ—DC #1

(1)	(2)			(3)	
	Monthly analysis			Year-to-date analysis	
Weeks of inventory available at DC at time of air shipments	Air freight $(000)	Cumulative total air freight $ (000)	Cumulative percent of month's air freight	Air freight $ (000)	Cumulative total air freight $ (000)	Cumulative percent of year's air freight
Greater than 8	$ -	$ -	0 %	$250	$250	54%
Between 7 and 8	$ -	$ -	0 %	$20	$270	58%
Between 6 and 7	$ 1	$ 1	20 %	$30	$300	64%
Between 5 and 6	$ -	$ 1	20 %	$15	$315	67%
Between 4 and 5	$ -	$ 1	20 %	$2	$317	68%
Between 3 and 4	$ -	$ 1	20 %	$20	$337	72%
Between 2 and 3	$ -	$ 1	20 %	$60	$397	85%
Less than 2	$ 4	$ 5	100 %	$70	$467	100%

Table 13.2 Detailed analysis of air freight by product and by shipment

(Shipment to DC #1 from MM/DD to MM/DD—on normal ocean lanes)

(1)	(2)	(3)	(4)	(5)	(6)	(7)	(8)	(9) At time of air shipment:		(10)
Product name	Origin	Shipment number	Carrier	Ship Date	Units shipped	Air freight cost	Normal ocean cost	Weeks of inventory available at DC	Units of inventory available at DC	Units shipped to customers in previous 3 weeks
Widget 1	Plant A	abc 001			2000	$6,000	$1,000	8	16000	3000
Widget 2	Plant A	abc 002			1500	$6,500	$1,400	2	3500	5200
Widget 3	Plant A	abc 003			1000	$7,000	$1,500	2	3000	4500
Widget 4	Plant B	def 001			2500	$5,500	$1,800	10	5000	1500
Widget 5	Plant B	def 002			2000	$6,000	$1,600	2	4000	6000
Widget 6	Plant B	def 003			1500	$7,000	$1,500	3	1000	1500
TOTAL						$38,000	$8,800			

155

would be for the appropriate managers to investigate this situation and determine whether corrective action is required.

Table 13.2 represents a more detailed monitoring report that facilitates a closer investigation if an issue is first identified using the summary report (Table 13.1). This second table provides the necessary item and shipment level detail on individual air shipments.

Note that column (9) indicates both the weeks of inventory (i.e., forward coverage) that was available at a DC when an air shipment occurred and the units of inventory available. Because this report provides transaction-level reporting, it allows managers to evaluate individual decisions made to utilize air freight. For example, was the inventory of a specific product in short supply at a DC when an air shipment was made, or was the DC already in a strong forward coverage inventory position at the time of the air shipment? This detailed analysis facilitates effective evaluation and decision making as to whether the firm must address inefficient use of air freight or whether it is employing air freight sensibly. Because Table 13.2 provides transaction-level detail, managers will typically need to review this analysis frequently (e.g., weekly or monthly) to utilize it productively. The data in Table 13.2 indicates that during a recent reporting period, two of the six total air shipments to DC #1 occurred in cases where the DC already had 8 or more weeks' forward inventory coverage (specifically, the shipments of widgets 1 and 4). This finding highlights unnecessary use of air freight, and a firm's managers can utilize this analysis to quickly address whether changes in scheduling procedures are required.

Monitoring Outbound Transportation Decisions: A Local Depot Example

To further illustrate the importance of transportation monitoring systems for network operations, we extend our example of Firm XYZ to consider outbound shipments to customers. Returning to Figure 13.1, we see that Firm XYZ's two-echelon DC network distributes finished goods to U.S. customers. Echelon 1 consists of the three regional DCs located across the United States. Echelon 2 consists of a series of small local transshipment points called local depots that receive deliveries from the regional DCs. These local depots receive truckload deliveries, sort and segregate these shipments, and then deliver these shipments to local customers. The shipments from XYZ's regional DCs contain many small individual customer orders that XYZ ships as one full truckload to its local depots to minimize freight costs.

To facilitate effective order cycle times to its customers, Firm XYZ must maintain a good frequency of shipments between its regional DCs and its local transshipment points or depots (e.g., a full truckload at least every other day or, ideally, on a daily basis). In establishing its two-echelon DC outbound network, Firm XYZ did an analysis to select local depot locations where enough demand existed to generate DC-to-depot truckload shipments of at least three per week. Now, XYZ must monitor its network to ensure that it achieves the DC-to-depot shipment frequency that it planned. Table 13.3 illustrates a standard diagnostic report that assists Firm XYZ to monitor its network. Based on a rolling 12-week historical period, this table compares:

- the average shipments per week between regional DCs and local depots versus planned shipments,
- the planned average weight per shipment versus actual, and
- the planned average freight cost per pound versus actual.

From this analysis, Firm XYZ's planners can quickly observe that the tonnage and frequency of shipments between a regional DC and local depot #4 have been significantly below plan for the last 12 weeks. Column (3) indicates that local depot #4 has received an average of only two shipments per week during this time. Further, column (4) reveals that the average weight of shipments to depot #4 are also significantly under plan, and this translates to a higher cost per pound than planned (column 5). In addition, longer average cycle times result from a frequency of only two shipments per week. In summary, Table 13.3 highlights that Firm XYZ has a service and cost issue to address at local depot #4.

Summary

In this chapter, we described several methods for monitoring and controlling transportation activities. We provided three brief illustrations of the type of diagnostic tools and reports that firms' operating manufacturing

Table 13.3 Illustrative operational monitoring and feedback system

(1)	(2)	(3)		(4)			(5)		
Transshipment point or local warehouse	Number of shipments from regional warehouse to local warehouse during last 12 weeks	Average shipments per week from regional warehouse to local warehouse		Average lbs. per shipment			Average freight cost per lb.		
		Planned	Actual	Planned	Actual		Actual	Planned	Actual
1	55	5.0	5.5	36,000	37,000		37,000	$ 0.04	$ 0.04
2	50	5.0	5.0	35,000	38,000		38,000	$ 0.03	$ 0.03
3	30	3.0	3.0	37,000	40,000		40,000	$ 0.04	$ 0.04
4	20	3.0	2.0	35,000	17,000		17,000	$ 0.04	$ 0.08
5	45	4.0	4.5	35,000	36,000		36,000	$ 0.03	$ 0.03
• • •	• • •	• • •	• • •	• • •	• • •		• • •	• • •	• • •
Total/Average									

and distribution networks should have in place to monitor short-term and long-term logistics operations. Using the tools presented, we showed how a firm identified opportunities to improve its air-versus-ocean modal decision making on inbound replenishments to its DCs, as well as its outbound service and costs to customers in a specific region. Particularly on large-scale networks, firms must have readily available analytics-based decision support such as those illustrated in this chapter in order to ensure effective and efficient operations. In the absence of this type of decision support, operational inefficiencies and substandard customer service may exist for months and years on a network, but not be fully recognized by a firm.

Part Three: Summary and Conclusion

In Part Three, we have addressed how to apply metrics and other techniques for monitoring and controlling logistics operations. We presented a hierarchical framework for organizing logistics metrics and applied this framework to specific logistics functions. We showed how this framework accommodates metrics that are external, focusing on effectiveness, and internal, focusing on efficiency. We then created a customized index to monitor overall logistics operations. We offered several approaches for determining the weights of the metrics included in the index, including the AHP, which facilitates developing a consensus across the logistics management team. We completed our discussion by presenting some DSS tools for monitoring and controlling inbound and outbound transportation activities. We first considered inbound plant-to-DC transportation modal decisions, in order to verify that the more expensive transportation mode (air) is used only when weeks of available inventory are below an established threshold. Finally, we addressed outbound cost and service issues that arise with DC-to-depot truckload shipments.

The framework and monitoring and control methods presented in this chapter will enable logistics managers to ensure that their operations continue to meet performance expectations by providing the necessary information to address any shortfalls that might occur. In Part Three, we illustrated these management tools for just a few of the many logistics operations to which managers can and should apply them. However, these represent techniques and methods that are applicable to virtually all logistics operations.

CHAPTER 14

Final Thoughts on Logistics Analytics and Decision Support

In this book, we have presented numerous frameworks, decision support systems, and analytics methods to facilitate effective and efficient logistics decision making. These collective tools enhance a logistics organization's success in meeting its customers' and suppliers' needs (i.e., to operate effectively), while at the same time minimizing its costs and maximizing its profitability (i.e., to operate efficiently). While the topics presented represent just a portion of all the methodologies available today, they do cover a broad swath of the logistics analytics decision support tools that logistics professionals should utilize on a regular basis. Further, the methodologies presented here can, in many cases, be readily adapted to other logistics activities and decisions not explicitly addressed in this book.

Our discussion of logistics analytics began with a review of transportation mode choice decision making in Part One. After first considering how transportation decisions fit into an overall strategic, tactical, and operational planning hierarchy, we focused on an integrated inventory and transportation mode selection approach. This methodology explicitly incorporates the impact of transportation mode choice on a firm's inventory investment requirements. We observed that in establishing its mode strategy for major transportation lanes on its network, a firm must evaluate how inventory requirements and inventory costs differ under alternative supply replenishment modes (e.g., air vs. ocean). Our analytics methodology demonstrated that firms that neglect to consider inventory costs in the transport mode selection process, risk making highly inefficient decisions. Finally, in Part One, we illustrated all the equations of our transport mode choice methodology so that other logistics practitioners can easily build their own version of this spreadsheet-based system for their firm's use.

Part Two covered a broad set of logistics functions, including manufacturing, warehouse operations, and inventory management. We reviewed several case studies where firms employed optimization, simulation, large-scale databases, and related analytics tools to guide their strategic, tactical, and operational planning and scheduling decisions. Additionally, we reviewed several key decision support tools such as feedback loops and activity-based costing that our industry experience indicates are critical yet often underinvested in by logistics organizations.

One underlying theme of our discussions was that it is important for a logistics organization to standardize the use of its analytics decision support tools and frameworks as regularly scheduled business processes. As an example, we described how CPFR has, over several decades, become an industry standard for many logistics planning activities between firms. However, CPFR originated from a small, informal, collaborative forecasting experiment between Walmart and Warner-Lambert. Over time, the standardization of this initial process set the stage for an extraordinary expansion and mass acceptance of this and related CPFR methodologies across many industries.

In Part Three, we reviewed an assortment of analytics techniques and a hierarchical metrics framework to facilitate the monitoring and control of logistics operations. We observed the value of organizing a firm's logistics metrics into a linked hierarchy of strategic, tactical, and operational measures. This approach of utilizing a hierarchical planning framework for major logistics functions, whether it be manufacturing operations, distribution, transportation, performance measurement, or others represents another key theme emphasized throughout the book. We also briefly described the AHP and the concept of building customized indices to monitor logistics operations. References were provided for practitioners wishing to explore the AHP and customized indices in more depth. Finally, we presented some DSS tools for monitoring and controlling inbound and outbound transportation activities.

In conclusion, we have attempted to share many of the logistics analytics decision support methods and tools that have ably assisted numerous logistics professionals, including the authors. We encourage logistics practitioners to utilize these and other analytics tools on a regular basis. They lead to better logistics decision making.

References

Bowersox, D.J., D.J. Closs, M.B. Cooper, and J.C. Bowersox. 2013. *Supply Chain Logistics Management.* 4th ed. New York, NY: McGraw-Hill.

Brealey, R.A., S.C. Myers, and F. Allen. 2017. *Principles of Corporate Finance.* 12th ed. New York, NY: McGraw-Hill.

Chea, A. 2011. "Activity-Based Costing System in the Service Sector: A Strategic Approach for Enhancing Managerial Decision Making and Competitiveness." *International Journal of Business and Management* 6, no.11, pp. 3–10.

Cooper, R., and R.S. Kaplan, 1988. "Measure Costs Right: Make the Right Decisions." *Harvard Business Review* 66, no. 5, pp. 96–103.

Coyle, J.C., C.J. Langley, Jr., R.A. Novack, and B.J. Gibson. 2017. *Supply Chain Management: A Logistics Perspective.* 10th ed. Boston, MA: Cengage Learning.

Datapine, 2019. *Dashboard Examples.* www.datapine.com/dashboard-examples-and-templates/logistics, (accessed September 10, 2019).

Evers, P.T., and F.J. Beier. 1993. "The Portfolio Effect and Multiple Consolidation Points: A Critical Assessment of the Square Root Law". *Journal of Business Logistics* 14, no. 2, pp. 109–25.

Expert Choice. 2019. *Expert Choice Solutions – How AHP Works.* www.expertchoice.com/ahp-software, (accessed September 10, 2019).

GS1 US. 2019. *GS1 US.* www.gs1us.org, (accessed September 10, 2019).

Gupta, V., E. Peters, T. Miller, and K. Blyden. 2002. "Implementing a Distribution Network Decision Support System at Pfizer/Warner-Lambert." *Interfaces* 32, no. 4, pp. 28–45.

Hax, A.C., and H.C. Meal., 1975. "Hierarchical Integration of Production Planning and Scheduling." In *Studies in Management Sciences, Logistics 1*, ed. M.A. Geisler. Amsterdam, The Netherlands: North Holland.

Liberatore, M., 1987. "An Extension of the Analytic Hierarchy Process for Industrial R&D Project Selection and Resource Allocation." *IEEE Transactions on Engineering Management* 34, no. 1, pp. 12–18.

Liberatore, M.J., and T. Miller, 1998. "A Framework for Integrating Activity Based Costing and the Balanced Scorecard into the Logistics Strategy Development and Monitoring Process." *Journal of Business Logistics*, 19, no. 2, pp. 131–54.

Liberatore, M., and T. Miller, 2012. *Supply Chain Planning: Practical Frameworks for Superior Performance.* New York, NY: Business Expert Press.

Liberatore, M., T. Monahan, and D. Stout, 1992. "A Framework for Integrating Capital Budgeting Analysis with Strategy." *The Engineering Economist* 38, no. 1, pp. 31–43.

Maister, D.H. 1976. "Centralization of Inventories and the 'Square Root Law'." *International Journal of Physical Distribution* 6, no. 3, pp. 124–34.

Miller, T. 1991. "A Note on Integrating Current End Item Inventory Conditions into Optimization Based Long Run Aggregate Production and Distribution Planning Activities." *Production and Inventory Management Journal* 32, no. 4, pp. 74–80.

Miller, T. 2002. *Hierarchical Operations and Supply Chain Management.* 2nd Ed. London: Springer-Verlag Press.

Miller, T. 2009. "Notes on Using Optimization and DSS Techniques to Support Supply Chain and Logistics Operations." In *Optimization and Logistics Challenges in the Enterprise*, eds. W. Chaovalitwongse, K.C. Furman, and P.M. Pardalos. New York, NY: Springer, pp. 191–210.

Miller, T. 2006. *Strategic Logistics: Efficient Transportation Decisions.* Allegan, MI: Boskage Commerce Publications.

Miller, T. 2016. "Supply Chain Frameworks: A Constant In The Midst Of Change." In *Supply Chain Management and Logistics: Innovative Strategies and Practical Solutions*, eds. Zhe Liang, Art Chaovalitwongse, and Leyuan Shi. Boca Raton, FL: CRC Press.

Miller, T. 2017. "The ABCs of Activity Based Costing for Logistics". *Materials Handling and Logistics Magazine.* July/August, pp. 22–5.

Miller, T., R. De Matta, and M. Xu. 2016. "High Level Inventory Network Modeling Approaches". In *The Handbook of Research on Global Supply Chain Management*, ed. Bryan Christiansen. Hershey, PA: IGI Global, pp. 15–44.

Miller, T., and M. Liberatore, 2011. "A Practical Framework for Supply Chain Planning." *Supply Chain Management Review* 15, no. 2, pp. 38–44.

Miller, T., E. Peters, O. Bode, and V. Gupta. 2013. "A Logistics Deployment Decision Support System at Pfizer". *Annals of Operations Research*, 203, pp. 81–99.

Miller, T., and S. Smith, 2011. "Integrate Network Design and Warehouse Design," *Materials Handling and Logistics Magazine*, February, pp. 50–2.

Quintanilla, G. 2018. *In Supply Chain News*. www.supplychain247.com/article/ what_are_supply_chain_professionals_using_to_make_network_ decisions/aimms?ajs_uid=8353H9976923D9C&oly_enc_ id=8353H9976923D9C&ajs_trait_oebid=8232A5796912A4H, (accessed November 7, 2018).

Saaty, T.L. 1996. *The Analytic Hierarchy Process*. Pittsburgh, PA: RWS Publications.

Super Decisions. 2019. www.superdecisions.com, (accessed September 10, 2019).

Supply Chain 24/7. 2019. *VICS Company Profile*. www.supplychain247. com/company/voluntary_interindustry_commerce_solutions, (accessed October 3, 2019).

Tyagi, R., and C. Das. 1998. "Extension of the Square Root Law for Safety Stock to Demands with Unequal Variances." *Journal of Business Logistics* 19, no.2, pp. 197–204.

Zinn, W., M. Levy, and D.J. Bowersox. 1989. "Measuring the Effect of Inventory Centralization/Decentralization on Aggregate Safety Stock: The 'Square Root Law' Revisited." *Journal of Business Logistics* 10, no. 1, pp. 1–14.

About the Authors

Tan Miller, PhD, is a professor and the director of the supply chain management program at Rider University. Previously he was responsible for the operations of Johnson & Johnson's US Consumer Distribution Network. He also has headed the U.S. Consumer Healthcare Logistics Network of Pfizer, and held positions with Mercer Management Consulting, Unisys, Warner-Lambert, and American Olean Tile Company. Tan has published extensively on logistics, and received an MA, MBA and PhD degrees from the University of Pennsylvania.

Matthew J. Liberatore, PhD, is the John F. Connelly chair in management at the Villanova School of Business, Villanova University. He previously served as associate dean, management department chair and director of the Center for Business Analytics. He also held management positions at FMC Corporation. Matt has published extensively in supply chain management, operations research/analytics, information systems, project management and health care decision making, and received BA, MS and PhD degrees from the University of Pennsylvania.

Index

OTHER TITLES IN OUR SUPPLY AND OPERATIONS MANAGEMENT COLLECTION

Joy M. Field, Boston College, *Editor*

- *The Practical Guide to Transforming Your Company by* Daniel Plung and Connie Krull
- *Production Line Efficiency: A Comprehensive Guide for Managers* by Sabry Shaaban and Sarah Hudson
- *Transforming US Army Supply Chains: Strategies for Management Innovation* by Greg Parlier
- *Orchestrating Supply Chain Opportunities: Achieving Stretch Goals, Efficiently* by Ananth Iyer and Alex Zelikovsky
- *Design, Analysis and Optimization of Supply Chains: A System Dynamics Approach* by William Killingsworth
- *Supply Chain Planning and Analytics: The Right Product in the Right Place at the Right Time* by Gerald Feigin
- *Supply-Chain Survival in the Age of Globalization* by James A. Pope
- *Better Business Decisions Using Cost Modeling: For Procurement, Operations, and Supply Chain Professionals* by Victor Sower and Christopher Sower
- *Supply Chain Risk Management: Tools for Analysis* by David Olson
- *Leading and Managing the Lean Management Process* by Gene Fliedner
- *Supply Chain Information Technology* by David Olson
- *Managing Commodity Price Risk: A Supply Chain Perspective* by George A Zsidisin Bowling and Janet Hartley
- *Global Supply Chain Management* by Matt Drake
- *Improving Business Performance With Lean* by James Bradley
- *RFID for the Supply Chain and Operations Professional* by Pamela Zelbst and Victor Sower
- *Sustainability Delivered: Designing Socially and Environmentally Responsible Supply Chains* by Madeleine Pullman and Margaret Sauter

Announcing the Business Expert Press Digital Library

Concise e-books business students need for classroom and research

This book can also be purchased in an e-book collection by your library as

- *a one-time purchase,*
- *that is owned forever,*
- *allows for simultaneous readers,*
- *has no restrictions on printing, and*
- *can be downloaded as PDFs from within the library community.*

Our digital library collections are a great solution to beat the rising cost of textbooks. E-books can be loaded into their course management systems or onto students' e-book readers. The **Business Expert Press** digital libraries are very affordable, with no obligation to buy in future years. For more information, please visit **www.businessexpertpress.com/librarians**. To set up a trial in the United States, please email **sales@businessexpertpress.com**.